T0212588

The
ISO 9000
Implementation
Manual

The ISO 9000 Implementation Manual

Ten Steps to ISO 9000 Registration

Greg Hutchins

omneo

AN IMPRINT OF OLIVER WIGHT PUBLICATIONS, INC.
85 Allen Martin Drive
Essex Junction, VT 05452

Copyright 1994 by Greg Hutchins

Published by Oliver Wight Publications, Inc.

All rights reserved. This book or any parts thereof may not be reproduced without permission from the publisher.

Oliver Wight Publications books may be purchased for educational, business, or sales promotional use. For information, please call or write: Special Sales Department, Oliver Wight Publications, Inc., 85 Allen Martin Drive, Essex Junction, VT 05452. Telephone: (800) 343-0625 or (802) 878-8161; FAX: (802) 878-3384.

Library of Congress Catalog Card Number: 93-061774

ISBN: 0-939246-63-5

Text design by Irving Perkins Associates

2 4 6 8 10 9 7 5 3 1

CONTENTS

LIST OF FIGURES

PREFACE

The expression "times are changing" has never been more true than it is today. Organizations are facing excruciating external competitive pressures. As customers' expectations are rising, costs are being slashed, business units are being sold, and people are being fired. Change is often leading to organizational turmoil: organizations and employees are asking where are they going and how are they going to get there profitably. Adding to these pressures is the requirement—or, as some would say, the opportunity—to become ISO 9000 registered.

This book is for those of you who have to register as a result of a competitive requirement, regulatory compliance, or customer mandate. Whatever your motivation, the result is the same: ISO 9000 registration has become a condition of business. It is something that you *have to do* in order to stay in business—in other words, to survive.

In some ways, ISO 9000 implementation and registration is new in the United States, even though since 1987 it's been widespread in Europe. Current U.S. ISO 9000 registration growth can be described only as explosive: it is doubling and even tripling each year.

In many ways, ISO 9000 registration and implementation are still largely untested territory. U.S. service providers and regulatory authorities have had to play catch-up. Registrars have had to develop uniform registration rules and standardize auditor quality. Governments have had to determine what role they will play in certifying auditors and accrediting registrars.

TO IMPLEMENT QUALITY SYSTEMS OR BECOME
ISO 9000 REGISTERED

The decision to implement ISO 9000 is independent of registration. A company can achieve some of the benefits of ISO 9000 implementation without going through the registration process. In many organizations, ISO 9000 management and operational concepts can be implemented as part of a reorganizing or reengineering initiative.

ISO 9000 implementation or registration is only one step in the competitiveness journey. Some consultants call the journey *continuous improvement* (CI) or *total quality management* (TQM). Some feel that ISO 9000 registration is the ultimate goal for any organization. ISO 9000 registration *is* important, but it is only one step on an organization's continuous improvement journey to position itself for competitiveness. For some organizations, it may be a giant step, for others a bureaucratic step, and for even others simply a documentation step.

A more progressive view is to see ISO 9000 quality systems implementation as an important tool of competitiveness. ISO 9000 registration is not the journey's end. ISO 9000 registration is an important, independent validation that quality systems have been successfully implemented. This book focuses on describing how to become registered, but its implicit message is that implementing quality systems is a valuable means of increasing competitiveness.

BENEFITS DRIVEN

What will this book do for you? This book will help you to

1. Understand the basics of ISO 9000 implementation and registration,

2. Follow a simple and practical series of steps to become registered,

3. Identify opportunities to save money,

4. Suggest ways to improve your operations, and

5. Suggest ways to use ISO 9000 registration to satisfy your customers.

Will this book guarantee your registration? No. But it will point you in the right direction. This book provides tips, resources, suggestions, strategies, and tactics to guide you through the registration process as well as to help you stay registered.

By following the step-by-step approach detailed in this book, chances are good that you'll achieve registration and maintain it—something that is almost as difficult as becoming registered. The registrar who audits you biyearly or yearly will require that you maintain and improve quality systems. The challenge is to overcome the postregistration blues—the relaxing of efforts that often occurs when something demanding has been accomplished, such as successful ISO 9000 registration.

WHO SHOULD READ THIS BOOK?

The ISO 9000 Implementation Manual can be used by any organization in almost any industry sector—large, small, public, or private. This book will be particularly useful to medium and small organizations that don't have extensive resources or external consultants.

This book is a practical, how-to-become-registered book. It details a systematic approach to ISO 9000 registration. The project, systems, and team-based approaches to ISO 9000 registration are highly integrated and address the major points of ISO 9000 registration.

ISO 9000 registration does not require superhuman effort, just consistent effort. If you thumb through this book, you'll see that the suggestions focus on common-sense suggestions and follow largely a linear path. The ISO 9000 Implementation Manual covers more material than you may need to become registered, but you should be familiar with and consider most, if not all, the points and issues raised in this book.

Is this the only way to become registered? No. My goal is to explain how to get started and how to stay on the registration path. It's important to customize your ISO 9000 registration to fit your needs and requirements. I hope that this book fills the void between academic registration treatises and the "this is the way I became registered" experiences of specific organizations.

Good luck and have fun.

Greg Hutchins
(800) COMPETE™

INTRODUCTION

Any business activity involves addressing and answering these seemingly simple questions:

1. Where are you going?
2. Why are you going there?
3. How are you going to get there?
4. Who's going to facilitate the effort?
5. What road map are you going to follow?
6. What are the milestones along the way?

Although the questions are simple, finding answers is difficult. In this book, we're going to become ISO 9001/9002/9003 registered. The process for pursuing both ISO 9001 and ISO 9003, is fairly similar. The major difference is that ISO 9001 has twenty quality system requirements for demonstrating compliance, while ISO 9003 has twelve quality system requirements.

This book addresses questions 2 through 6 in the above list, particularly the important second question, "Why are you going there?" The rationale for and benefits of ISO 9000 registration or quality systems implementation must be understood to develop organizational consensus and then dedicate resources to ensure its success.

In this book, the steps that lead to registration are sequential, but many can be accomplished at the same time. The parallel effort is called *simultaneous* or *concurrent ISO 9000 registration*; its goal is to shorten the preparation and documentation timeline.

THE THREE BASIC BUSINESS APPROACHES

This book is anchored in three fundamental business approaches: the systems approach, project management approach, and the team approach.

THE SYSTEMS APPROACH

In business, the systems approach is a method for describing integrative processes. Flexible, multidisciplinary teams are used as the mechanism for attaining organizational objectives—in this case, ISO 9000 registration. Project management techniques promote the orderly organizing, planning, scheduling, managing, controlling, and financing of the ISO 9000 registration project using available resources.

The systems approach also is used to structure ISO 9000. ISO 9000 is a family of quality systems documents that offer an organization the prescriptive and descriptive means (called *quality systems*) for pleasing customers, satisfying contractual requirements, and becoming more efficient.

This book follows a systems approach to ISO 9000 registration and maintenance because the approach implements ISO 9000 quality systems in an integrated and unified fashion across many different functional areas and organization sites. The specific ISO 9000 benefits delivered by the systems approach are that it

- Offers a disciplined and logical process for arriving at a decision or objective and facilitates describing and understanding the interrelationships of ISO 9000 implementation,

- Lends itself well to both the project and team-based approaches to registration,

- Allows quality processes to be easily and logically described, and

- Allows interrelationships among process steps to be easily described.

The Project Management Approach

The registration process is a project-oriented process: it requires getting something done successfully on time and within budget. It involves all the elements of a successful project—particularly management functions such as planning, monitoring, controlling, analyzing, and reporting.

Project management techniques lend themselves to achieving ISO 9000 registration objectives because the registration process

- Is an integrated process,
- Has a specific objective,
- Has definite start and end dates,
- Follows a specific series of steps,
- Requires leadership and team organization,
- Uses resources in an efficient manner,
- Identifies functional areas and team responsibilities,
- Identifies time limits and facilitates establishing schedules,
- Identifies timelines and project benchmarks, and
- Facilitates corrective action.

The Team Approach

Teams have been used successfully in project planning, product development, construction projects, quality improvement, sales enhancement, and other special activities. Experience has shown that interacting groups show superior performance. Why? Teams allow for many different points of view to be articulated and shared. Team members are more apt to invest emotionally in a team project than in traditional top-down management-dictated projects. Teams promote consensus decision making: everyone's views are heard, and everyone is involved in planning, implementation, and results monitoring.

The advantages of using the project team approach to ISO 9000 registration and maintenance are that this approach

- Improves internal communication,

- Improves reaction time,

- Encourages operational investment,

- Facilitates problem solving, and

- Allows for easier development of procedures.

IS THERE ONE RIGHT WAY?

Is there one right way to pursue ISO 9000 implementation or registration? No. But there are commonsensical approaches: ISO 9000 registration probably best follows a project approach; registration maintenance involves developing the right quality systems.

Managing any complex project—such as managing ISO 9000 registration to completion—is a difficult task. To many, ISO 9000 registration may be seen as just another project on top of the many already planned. Resources must be gathered and channeled to the appropriate locations and tasks. Management must participate actively. Employees must be convinced of the benefits. Projects must be prioritized because everyone already has too many things to do.

ORGANIZATION OF THIS BOOK

STEP 1: UNDERSTAND THE ISO 9000 REGISTRATION ENVIRONMENT

ISO 9000 registration is occurring in a global environment that is made up of your customers, your competitors, and the regulatory authorities of various countries. It's critical that each of these stakeholders' needs and pressures is understood. These issues form the background against which you can make a wise decision whether to pursue registration or to implement ISO 9000 quality systems.

STEP 2: DETERMINE THE BENEFITS AND CHALLENGES OF ISO 9000 REGISTRATION

ISO 9000 registration benefits and challenges are presented in this section. More than thirty benefits to registering or implementing quality systems are briefly discussed. Using this laundry list, you'll be able to determine whether registration or implementation is right for you and develop a consensus among internal and external stakeholders about the benefits for your organization.

STEP 3: SECURE MANAGEMENT COMMITMENT

Management must be committed to and actively participate in the registration project and not simply endorse the concept and then delegate its implementation to others. And when the first major problem arises, costs mount, and registration takes longer than anticipated, management must be prepared for organizational enthusiasm to wear thin and take steps to motivate employees for the long term. Management and the entire organization must understand and quantify both the short- and long-term benefits of implementation or registration. The success of this effort depends on the perceptions, attitudes, and expectations of the people who create and use the quality systems on a day-to-day basis.

STEP 4: PLAN FOR ISO 9000 REGISTRATION

Registration and implementation should be thoroughly planned, and strategic and tactical plans should be organization specific. This section contains planning checklists and tips that will guide and prepare you for the registration process.

STEP 5: ORGANIZE FOR REGISTRATION

The ISO 9000 registration team facilitates the registration and implementation processes. The team plans and implements quality systems and verifies that they are in place, operating properly, and fully documented. The team encourages and ensures participation by the entire organization throughout the project. The team ensures that registration is implemented on time and under budget and that it meets requirements.

STEP 6: TRAIN AND EDUCATE

ISO 9000 registration is often piggybacked onto other quality initiatives, such as creating a learning organization. Many organizations are discovering that continuous learning and adaptation are essential in a continuously changing economy. ISO 9000 quality systems implementation sometimes requires employees learn new methods, technologies, and skills.

STEP 7: CONDUCT THE PREASSESSMENT

The purpose of the preassessment is to determine the "what is" status of quality system implementation and documentation and to compare these against the "what shall be" as specified by ISO 9001/9002/9003. This is called ISO 9000 document gap analysis or simply *gap analysis*. A small gap means that less needs to be done to become registered; a large gap implies that more quality documentation needs to be developed.

STEP 8: DEVELOP QUALITY DOCUMENTATION

This section discusses the three levels of quality documentation that are usually evaluated—the quality manual, procedures, and work instructions. Developing quality documentation that complies with the specific requirements of ISO 9001/9002/9003 is the most time-consuming and expensive element of ISO 9000 registration. To develop site, organization, process, and work-specific procedures and instructions requires understanding what work is done in the organization and perhaps redesigning processes so that work can be done better and compliance with ISO 9001/9002/9003 is achieved.

STEP 9:   SELECT A REGISTRAR

Eighty or more percent of the registration effort is expended in planning and preparing for the registration assessment. If you've followed the process outlined in this book, you should be well prepared for the registration audit.

Because ISO 9000 registration is a partnership between the registrar and you, the registrar should be selected carefully. The major criteria, including costs, for selecting the registrar are discussed in this section. You may be spending many years with the registrar, so choose carefully.

STEP 10:   MAINTAIN REGISTRATION

ISO 9000 registration is a long-term process of continuous auditing to higher ISO 9000 quality system standards in order to be able to comply with ISO 9000 revisions. The registrar will audit you every six months or each year as part of the registration agreement. Because ISO 9000 registration is often used as the basis for sourcing decisions, it's critical that you maintain registration and improve your quality systems over time.

FIGURE 1.1
Registration Steps

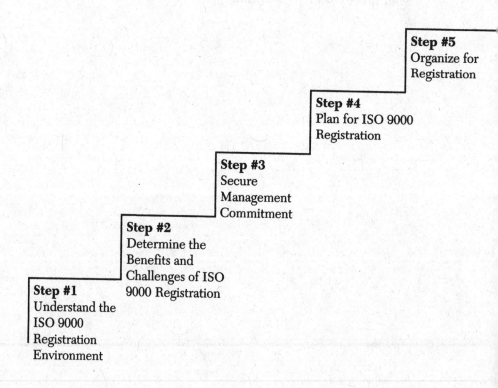

Step #5
Organize for
Registration

Step #4
Plan for ISO 9000
Registration

Step #3
Secure
Management
Commitment

Step #2
Determine the
Benefits and
Challenges of ISO
9000 Registration

Step #1
Understand the
ISO 9000
Registration
Environment

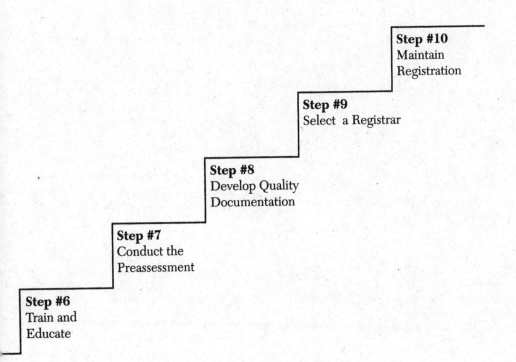

Step #10
Maintain
Registration

Step #9
Select a Registrar

Step #8
Develop Quality
Documentation

Step #7
Conduct the
Preassessment

Step #6
Train and
Educate

The
ISO 9000
Implementation
Manual

STEP 1

UNDERSTAND THE ISO 9000 REGISTRATION ENVIRONMENT

Key Steps
• Understand ISO 9000.
• Understand the benefits of implementation.
• Understand the benefits of registration.
• Define customer requirements.
• Identify ISO 9000 stakeholders.
• Identify each stakeholder's needs, wants, and requirements.
• Understand regulatory requirements.
• Understand marketplace and customer challenges and requirements.
• Understand the internal benefits of registration and implementation.

As the buzz about ISO 9000 registration has become a roar, a herd mentality about registration often emerges. People say, "I've heard that ISO 9000 registration is required to sell in Europe or in Mexico or to the U.S. government." Or "If so and so down the street is becoming registered, then this is something I've got to do." Let's look at the facts.

Although sometimes there is no compelling reason for an organization to register to ISO 9000, the me-too pressures, especially on small businesses, can be enormous. Small business owners are susceptible to these pressures because their daily focus is on making quality products and selling them at sometimes razor-thin margins. Survival is often an issue for the small or medium-size business that feels it must do whatever is necessary to please the customer or stay ahead of the competition, including registering to ISO 9000.

ISO 9000 is hot. Many may not know what it means or what it is intended to do, but management doesn't want to be left behind. It pursues registration because it believes that the customer or the market will soon require it.

BEGINNING THE REGISTRATION PROCESS

The most important issue surrounding registration is to *understand and identify the benefits of ISO 9000 registration.* Talk to as many people as you can about the value of this effort. You need to understand and measure its value to your stakeholders—who may be direct customers or regulatory agencies.

The first and second steps in the registration process are closely linked. All organizations pursuing registration should understand why they are doing it and what's in it for them at journey's end. During the process step described in this section (Step 1), you will examine the background conditions and pressures that have led your organization to seek ISO 9000 registration. Step 2 outlines the major benefits and challenges of ISO 9000 registration and implementation.

HOW NOT TO PURSUE REGISTRATION

Two factors—customers and competitors—often drive the registration process. To satisfy customers or to develop a competitive advantage, a company may decide to pursue registration to

- Enter new markets,

- Press a promotional advantage,

- Take a positioning advantage, or

- Neutralize competition.

A company may pursue registration for motives not fully understood or articulated. Registration may be pursued because a small business owner wants to be the first in an industry sector, region, or city to achieve it. Ego is difficult to quantify in terms of value enhancement, but it is a real driver of many business decisions.

An organization shouldn't adopt or pursue registration on a whim or for ego gratification. Registration is a cost. In today's constrained economic times, ISO 9000 registration competes with other projects for scarce corporate resources. Inevitably, top management provides the registration mandate and articulates its purpose and benefits to the organization. Functional organizational areas also must support the process because they'll be responsible for maintaining them once they are implemented.

TO REGISTER OR NOT TO REGISTER

If you don't have customers or competitors forcing registration, you're probably asking, "Why pursue it?" Do you have quality problems resulting in sales loss, customer dissatisfaction, or operational inefficiencies? Poor internal quality, low productivity, and inefficiencies are major reasons for implementing ISO 9000. ISO 9000 quality systems implementation should make you more efficient and effective and lower costs.

Probably the most important issue surrounding registration is economic. Is registration or implementation going to save or make you money? Every firm has its own basis for analyzing economic problems and for determining economic return. Registration is not cheap, but it should pay for itself.

We're already seeing a minor backlash to ISO 9000 registration as some companies are asking, "Why are we doing this?" You may discover you may not want to register after all. That's fine. This book will have saved you money.

The decision to ISO 9000 register may involve many other factors. In the initial process of evaluating whether to register, the following background issues must be considered:

- Do you produce regulated products?

- Are customers requiring registration?

- Are your competitors registering?

- Will registration or implementation help you to become more efficient and productive?

Each of the above points is discussed in the following pages.

REGISTRATION OF REGULATED PRODUCTS

Do you produce regulated products? Regulated products may include natural gas appliances, medical devices, construction equipment, telecommunications equipment, and so on. National regulatory authorities require ISO 9000 quality systems registration or product certification of safety, health, and environmental products.

What are national regulatory authorities? Every industrial nation is responsible for the welfare of its citizens, and authorizes government agencies to administer and regulate specific industrial products. In the United States, the Food and Drug Administration regulates medical devices, and the Federal Communications Commission regulates communications equipment. These authorities set standards and specify compliance requirements for products certifying to these standards.

List of Regulated Industries Considering ISO 9000 Registration

The following is a partial list of regulated industries requiring or considering some form of certification, including ISO 9000 registration:

- Pressure vessels

- Construction products

- Natural gas appliances

- Medical devices

- Electromagnetic emission devices

- Elevators

- Fasteners

- Measurement and test equipment

- Telecommunications equipment

CUSTOMER REQUIREMENTS

Customers often drive the ISO 9000 registration process. A customer may require or strongly recommend that existing or prospective suppliers pursue ISO 9000 registration. But customers or other stakeholders may have different levels of interest in ISO 9000 registration. A customer may require a supplier to register as a condition of doing business—for the supplier to be included on (or even to be *considered* to be included on) the approved bidder's list. This is occurring in different industry sectors, including the auto industry, which is using harmonized ISO 9000 requirements to evaluate suppliers for sourcing decisions. A customer may recommend that the supplier pursue registration or require the supplier to provide product information, performance information, design calculations, or product certifications.

Who is the customer? The customer may be any stakeholder mandating or recommending ISO 9000 compliance. The customer may be the immediate buyer of a product, the buyer that is two or more tiers up the customer-supplier chain, or a governmental agency that regulates products. Most often, the company that is signing the purchase order requires ISO 9000 compliance.

CUSTOMER-SUPPLIER REQUIREMENTS

More customers are requiring that suppliers have quality systems in place, operate them properly, and be documented before the supplier becomes a partner. These customer-supplier partnering efforts are similar in vertical industry sectors, such as health care, nuclear, automotive, aerospace, and defense because suppliers often develop industry-specific core competencies. Auto suppliers have design expertise and manufacturing equipment to satisfy auto requirements; pharmaceutical companies have experience complying with FDA requirements. Manufacturers primarily design and manufacture for customers in a vertical market segment.

Customer-supplier certification documents traditionally have specified quality, delivery, cost, technology, and service requirements. In the auto industry, Ford's Q-101 and GM's Target for Excellence quality certification standards were similar in scope and detail. Chrysler, Ford, General Motors, and truck manufacturers

---

ISO 9000 Stakeholders

Stakeholders, including the external customer, are usually the impetus to registration. Critical stakeholders include the following:

- *External customers*   The external customer may be the immediate company you supply product to or one further upstream. The final customer may be mandating ISO 9000 registration through its supplier network or value-adding chain.

- *Internal customers*   Internal customers may be a top manager or the user of a machine or finished part you produce. A fabrication plant, for example, may produce parts assembled by another plant. This internal customer may require registration as part of its customer-supplier certification effort or as a means of ensuring the high quality of the fabrication plant's product.

- *Regulatory authorities*   Regulatory authorities are also a stimulus for the ISO 9000 registration. U.S. regulatory authorities—such as the Food Drug Administration, the Nuclear Regulatory Commission, or the Department of Defense—are considering or adopting ISO 9000 as a supplier requirement.

- *Suppliers*   Suppliers are integral to the ISO 9000 registration effort. ISO 9001/9002/9003 are customer-supplier documents. An important quality system requirement is purchasing quality. This ISO 9000 quality system requires a supplier's supplier, also called subsuppliers, to control the quality of its purchased products.

---

also have developed a common standard similar to ISO 9001. Since many suppliers serve mainly the auto industry, it makes sense to have one quality standard with which all auto suppliers must comply.

Traditionally, each auto company audited its suppliers according to essentially the same criteria, which was redundant and costly. The solution was to develop common criteria that all industry suppliers could comply with, conduct one audit, and then list successful suppliers on a register. Customers could check the register to obtain assurance of the supplier's quality program.

REQUIREMENTS FROM UPSTREAM CUSTOMERS

ISO 9001/9002/9003 are customer-supplier documents. Does your customer or your customer's customer recommend or require ISO 9000 registration? It's critical to understand customer requirements all the way up the supplier chain.

It's fairly easy to understand the purchasing requirements of your immediate customer. But what if you supply only the fasteners used in subassemblies in a regulated product and are three or more suppliers removed from the final customer? Should you pursue registration? Maybe. You need to understand the requirements of the final product manufacturer, specifically in terms of ISO 9000 registration. You may be asked or required to pursue registration in the near future.

You can't avoid a customer's requirement for registration, but before beginning the registration process, understand customer requirements specifically. Does your customer require registration, or will the customer be satisfied with ISO 9000 implementation? The customer may require implementation, or it may be content to observe your progress toward implementation.

COMPETITIVE CHALLENGES

If your competitors are pursuing registration, there is a good chance you may be also. Why?

Companies register primarily for competitive or market advantage. A company may want the prestige that comes with being the first registered company in an industry sector. It may want to advertise its registration in promotions and ads. A supplier may want to use registration as a lever with a customer or to nullify a competitor's registration advantage.

Who is a competitor? Competition takes several forms. Competition may be direct industry competitors or companies wanting to enter your market, and they may be foreign or domestic companies. Competitive pressures also may come from national regulatory agencies that impose ISO 9000 registration as a requirement to enter their domestic markets.

ANALYZING THE COMPETITION: BENCHMARKING

First, understand your market and where your competition is in relation to ISO 9000 registration. Benchmarking, a form of competitive analysis, can help you analyze your competition by learning what a competitor is doing and how well it is doing it.

Benchmarking can identify whether the competition is pursuing registration, which may become the rationale and impetus for your registration. You can then truthfully say, "We have to become registered because the competition is using its registration to take business away from us." Benchmarking also can provide a vivid picture of what may occur if registration is not pursued.

Benchmarking can be either a one-shot or a continuous long-term process of measuring products, services, practices, processes, or systems against the best. "The best" can be the best in class, in the world, or in an industry segment. The comparison can be done against the toughest competitors or against leading companies in different industry segments. The latter is sometimes easier to accomplish because it avoids the ethical problems of competitive intelligence gathering.

Competitive Background Factors Surrounding ISO 9000 Registration

Setting the stage is critical in analyzing the competition. Let's examine the background factors that may be important to conducting competitive ISO 9000 analysis:

- *Legal requirements* A regulatory agency may require ISO 9000 registration or product testing, especially of products dealing with safety, health, and the environment, in order to sell products in a specific country. For example, the Europeans are seeking product or quality systems certification of many regulated products.

- *Political* The politics of market access is constantly changing. In this hemisphere, the goal of the North American Free Trade Agreement (NAFTA) was to open up the Canadian, U.S., and Mexican markets by lowering tariffs. There are similar efforts to open up other hemispherical markets and to harmonize technical standards.

- *Economic* Economic growth in overseas markets, especially in the Pacific Rim, is releasing a tremendous demand for U.S. products. Lowering trade barriers—in the belief it generates jobs—has become an important element of U.S. economic policy.

- *Technological* There are hundreds of dissimilar product standards throughout the world. When products are not compatible or interchangeable, these differing technological standards become a major trade barrier.

(continued on facing page)

**Competitive Background Factors Surrounding
ISO 9000 Registration (*continued*)**

- *Industry characteristics and requirements* Some industry sectors are rapidly harmonizing quality standards and are requiring ISO 9000 registration of industry suppliers.

- *Competitor characteristics* Companies are registering to obtain competitive and positioning advantages. They are shouting the advantages of ISO 9000 registration in ads, company brochures, and other documents.

- *Barriers to entry* Some countries are requiring registration before suppliers can enter their markets or be on an approved bidder's list for a government contract.

- *Competitor's history of commercialization* Competitors have different approaches to new business development. For example, a company may follow a preemptive, proactive, or reactive approach to registration. A company follows a preemptive approach to blindside a competitor by being one of the first companies to be registered. With a proactive approach, the advantages of registration are understood, but it's not yet required. A company following a reactive approach would register when the customer requires it as a condition of business.

- *Competitor's core competencies* Core competencies are those world-class abilities or areas that a company excels in. Core competencies distinguish or separate a company from its competition.

- *Strengthening one's competencies* Once a company identifies its own and its competitor's core competencies, then it can strengthen its own strengths and neutralize those of the competitor.

Benchmarking can benefit an organization by

- Identifying where you stand in terms of your competitor's being ISO 9000 registered,

- Identifying ISO 9000 practices to make operations more efficient, effective, or economic,

- Helping it to gain market position and leadership,

- Helping it to assist customer-supplier partnering, reengineering, or concurrent engineering,

- Identifying best ISO 9000 practices,

- Supplying information on how to use registration to competitive advantage,

- Identifying the most efficient, effective, and economic method for achieving registration,

- Providing sample quality documentation, including quality manual, procedures, and work instructions,

- Improving internal processes and products,

- Establishing internal quality systems and controls, and

- Enhancing product reliability.

CONDUCTING THE BENCHMARKING STUDY

Who should do the benchmarking? Some companies have used centralized benchmarking groups or even an operational department to do their ISO 9000 benchmarking. Some companies conduct benchmarking studies using functional managers and team members. With this process, functional managers are responsible for the studies and for using the information derived from the studies. They know the questions to ask and the problems to look for. Because functional managers usually aren't familiar with the technicalities of benchmarking, they can be given proper training in what to benchmark, whom to benchmark, and how to gather the right information.

Benchmarking can be done through several steps in the ISO 9000 process. Benchmarking done before registration can determine whether competitors have gained advantages; during registration it can determine the most efficient and effective steps to follow; and after registration it can be used to obtain ideas about how registration can be maintained.

INTERNAL BENEFITS

During the current revolution in how work is conducted, organizations have been restructuring to do work more efficiently. The following list outlines some of the major developments facing organizations:

- The requirement for sales and market share is pushing all companies to be competitive.

- Competitiveness means giving customers what they want faster.

- Customers want higher-quality, more appealing products at lower prices, delivered just in time and in a courteous and professional manner.

- All organizations are rethinking old assumptions and are restructuring.

- More products and services are outsourced to world-class suppliers.

- Organizations are flattening.

- Middle management and first-line supervision are evolving to become mentors and facilitators.

- Processes are being reengineered and proceduralized.

- Self-managed teams are responsible for more activities, including self-supervision.

EARLY WARNING SIGNS

How do you know whether your organization can benefit from implementing ISO 9000 quality systems? Quality problems resulting in sales loss, customer dissatisfaction, or operational inefficiencies are a major reason for implementing the ISO 9000 quality system without pursuing registration.

Companies develop competencies and specializations that help them distinguish themselves from their competitors. These core competencies may be in technology, distribution, manufacturing, marketing, or sales. Can ISO 9000 implementation help you develop your expertise or correct your operating deficiencies?

ISO 9000 implementation improves operations by restructuring, proceduralizing, and eliminating non-value-adding activities, such as

- Rework or scrap,

- Excessive inventory,

- Queues or waiting lines,

- Unnecessary handling,

- Duplication of effort, or

- Inefficient activities.

ISO 9000 AND REENGINEERING

Competitive pressures are forcing changes at an ever-dizzying speed, and what was acceptable yesterday is often not acceptable today. Terms like *responsiveness* and *high-velocity performance* are heard more and more. Processes are being reengineered. Process constraints are eliminated, and value must be added in each activity.

All organizations are restructuring to maintain competitiveness. Restructuring takes many forms, including supplier partnering, reengineering, outsourcing, developing self-managed teams, selling divisions, or eliminating middle management. Often, many of these methods are used simultaneously. ISO 9000 implementation or registration can assist these initiatives.

To become competitive, companies are totally redesigning their operations through process reengineering. Reengineering starts with the premise that the entire organization's mission must be rethought and if necessary redesigned. The reengineering process is comprehensive, reexamining managerial, social, supplier, and technical systems.

In reengineering, fundamental questions, such as these, are asked:

- What are the objectives of the process?

- How many steps are in the process?

- What are the key elements of the process?

- What adds value and what detracts value?

- How can the detracting elements be eliminated?

- How can the system be improved?

ISO 9000 PROCEDURALIZATION

Should an organization use ISO 9000 to lead or become the model for restructuring? There is no easy answer to this question, but the following discussion may shed some light.

ISO 9000 registration is simply a means of ensuring that the quality system requirements are met. This is normally accomplished by developing a hierarchical set of quality documentation. The highest level is the quality manual, then procedures, and finally work instructions. The structure of quality documentation details how work reflecting ISO 9000 requirements is accomplished. The process of developing and writing the documentation defines and, more important, proceduralizes how work is conducted.

Proceduralization must be done carefully. A poorly restructured and proceduralized organization can sever communication links, disrupt operations, cause resentments, lower job satisfaction, create new bureaucracies, create political turmoil, and in general result in total organizational discontent. In organizations with a high degree of technical personnel, such as a R&D laboratory, restructuring operations results in additional problems.

In general, ISO 9000 proceduralization works well in organizational environments where

- Repetitive tasks are common,

- Organization is progressive and adaptable,

- Regulatory requirements and regulations predominate,

- Risks of deficiencies or shutdowns are high, and

- Customer requirements are high.

If ISO 9000 is used as the sole means to instill an organizational quality culture, create massive reorganization, or downsize dramatically, problems will result. ISO 9000 is basically a technical system. Although it may be linked with organizational models of organizational change, that is not its function.

In the next Step, we discuss the specific benefits and challenge of ISO 9000 registration.

DETERMINE THE BENEFITS AND CHALLENGES OF ISO 9000 REGISTRATION

Key Steps
• Identify the customer and marketing benefits of registration and implementation.
• Identify the internal benefits of registration and implementation.
• Identify the customer and supplier benefits of registration and implementation.
• Identify registration and implementation challenges.

Consultants, the media, and others have declared that ISO 9000 registration will make your organization more efficient, effective, and economic. Customers expect registrars to provide a value-added service. Some of these claims are true, and some are hyperbole. You can be an aware consumer by understanding the benefits and costs of your decisions.

This section discusses the benefits and challenges of ISO 9000 registration. If you pursue registration or simply implement internal quality systems, understand why you are doing it and more specifically how it will make you more efficient, effective, and economical.

In the last section, we discussed the background issues surrounding registration. In this section, ISO 9000 implementation and registration benefits are discussed from three perspectives:

1. Customer and marketing,

2. Internal, and

3. Customer and supplier partnering.

You may not realize all the benefits presented here, but even a few benefits may justify registration or implementation. Some of the challenges and disadvantages of registration are discussed at the end of the section.

CUSTOMER AND MARKETING BENEFITS

Customer and marketing concerns probably drive the ISO 9000 registration process in the United States. Where there are more product and service suppliers than customers, ISO 9000 registration is an important means of differentiating oneself from the competition.

ISO 9000 registration provides many customer and marketing benefits. It

- Provides access to markets,

- Conveys commitment to partnering,

- Fulfills contract requirements,

- Establishes promotional credibility,

- Conveys operational and quality systems assurance,

- Ensures that new and existing products satisfy customers,

- Controls risks and exposure, and

- Neutralizes competition.

PROVIDES ACCESS TO MARKETS

Customers and national authorities are expecting or requiring ISO 9000 registration of product manufacturers and service providers. Many customers are requiring registration before a company is placed on an approved bidder's list. Increasingly, national authorities are requiring registration as a means of showing compliance with international, national, or industry standards. The natural gas appliance, telecommunications, nuclear power industries are all nationally regulated and are encouraging companies in their sectors to register.

CONVEYS COMMITMENT TO PARTNERING

ISO 9000 implementation and registration requires time and money. Because finite resources are expended in the pursuit of continuous improvement—a goal of all customers—customers see ISO 9000 registration as a value-adding commitment to quality, continuous improvement, and future partnering.

FULFILLS CONTRACT REQUIREMENTS

ISO 9000 registration is sometimes a contractual preference or requirement in government and commercial contracts. For contracts that deal with safety, environmental, and health-related products, the customer wants assurance that suppliers have minimum quality systems. Many believe that minimum quality systems eventually will be required by government and public contractors throughout the world.

ESTABLISHES PROMOTIONAL CREDIBILITY

Most markets are crowded with competing products. Since product positioning is critically important, ISO 9000 registration can help organizations distinguish themselves from the competition. ISO 9000 registration serves several important promotional uses. First, registration is used to differentiate suppliers. A company that advertises quality—by winning the Malcolm Baldrige National Quality Award, becoming Q101 certified, or becoming ISO 9000 registered—has a powerful tool for establishing market credibility. While winning the Malcolm Baldrige award indicates a company has a world-class quality system, ISO 9000 registration indicates the company has passed a rigorous third-party appraisal of its quality systems. These efforts prove to the customer that a company is committed to quality and to customer satisfaction.

CONVEYS OPERATIONAL AND QUALITY SYSTEMS ASSURANCE

ISO 9000 registration also indicates that quality systems are in place and operating properly in locations not easily accessible by the customer. For example, instead of sending a team to audit a Sri Lankan supplier, the customer may verify that the supplier is in an international ISO 9000 register with the assumption that the Sri Lankan supplier would have quality systems similar to those in place in the Portland, Oregon, location.

ENSURES THAT NEW AND EXISTING PRODUCTS SATISFY CUSTOMERS

Rapid product development is a requisite for survival. Customer and supplier teams are brought together to develop products rapidly. ISO 9000 registration implies that the supplier has

- Created an organizational structure and quality foundation for rapid product development,

- Proceduralized operations,

- Stabilized capable quality systems, and

- Controlled design changes.

CONTROLS RISKS AND EXPOSURE

As the marketplace becomes more complex and litigious, the name of the business game is to evaluate and minimize risks. The risk may involve an element of quality, such as meeting specifications. Although ISO 9000 quality systems registration does not guarantee that products are safe or reliable, the third-party evaluation does indicate that the supplier has spent time and effort to develop and maintain quality systems. If the systems are in place and operating properly, the customer can be assured that the output of these processes probably conforms to specifications.

NEUTRALIZES COMPETITION

Many companies are becoming registered because their competitors have done so. The competition may be using ISO 9000 registration for market positioning or to secure a contract where registration is a requirement. In today's competitive market, a slight advantage held by a competitor can tip a contract. And ISO 9000 registration does indicate a quality commitment.

INTERNAL BENEFITS

In many ways, ISO 9000 implementation results in more efficient, effective, and economic operations, but an organization can achieve ISO 9000 internal benefits without going through the registration process. It can gain benefits through proceduralizing, stabilizing, and improving its integral operations. Implementation

- Facilitates quality planning,
- Promotes a universal approach to quality,
- Can be used in many industries,
- Assists in establishing operational baselines,
- Operationalizes quality,
- Provides insights into organizational relationships,
- Develops self-discipline,

- Encourages an internal focus,

- Establishes production credibility,

- Facilitates internal operational control,

- Assists employees in understanding and improving operations,

- Encourages self-assessment,

- Maintains internal consistency,

- Controls processes and systems,

- Makes internal operations more efficient and effective,

- Ensures that product design changes are controlled,

- Creates an awareness of the need for training, and

- Encourages operational problem solving.

FACILITATES QUALITY PLANNING

ISO 9000 implementation encourages a company to plan how quality will be controlled throughout product development from concept to delivery. Quality planning specifically assists a company in

- Defining customer requirements,

- Outlining how quality is monitored and controlled,

- Ensuring design, process, installation, and serving compatibility,

- Identifying critical quality measurement equipment, and

- Ensuring proper quality documentation.

PROMOTES A UNIVERSAL APPROACH TO QUALITY

There are multiple approaches to total quality management deployment. Every consultant has his or her own definition of quality and set of quality principles, and numerous quality awards, standards, specifications, and other teachings promote still more definitions. In the face of this multiplicity of specifications, the confused customer can turn to ISO 9000 for a set of globally used definitions of quality management. ISO 9001/9002/9003 provide a set of universally accepted customer-supplier documents.

CAN BE USED IN MANY INDUSTRIES

ISO 9000 is a "one size fits all" family of documents. As generic documents, they can be used by small manufacturers as well as software houses. Universality is ISO 9000's biggest appeal, but it is also its greatest liability because it has to be tailored to the specific organization.

ASSISTS IN ESTABLISHING OPERATIONAL BASELINES

All organizations desire to be competitive and to optimize operations. But many companies still run on automatic pilot with an attitude that what was good enough yesterday is still good today. This complacency can be a recipe for disaster. By establishing baselines from which to reengineer or to improve operations, ISO 9000 implementation encourages

- Internal focus,
- Operational understanding, and
- Operational control.

OPERATIONALIZES QUALITY

Quality often is perceived as a department issue, especially in small organizations. There is no operational ownership of quality. ISO 9000 implementation results in proceduralized and operationalized quality by helping you

- Develop quality procedures and work instructions,
- Define quality authorities and responsibilities, and
- Make internal groups responsible for quality.

PROVIDES INSIGHTS INTO ORGANIZATIONAL RELATIONSHIPS

ISO 9000 incorporates closed-loop quality systems. Departments, suppliers, and other quality stakeholders must work together to ferret out and solve chronic and systemic problems. Some quality systems require a multifunctional and multi-departmental approach, including

- Internal auditing,
- Corrective action,
- Training, and
- Design review.

DEVELOPS SELF-DISCIPLINE

ISO 9000 implementation develops self-discipline by helping you to procedural-ize operations. The process of developing and writing procedures and work instructions compels an organization to understand what is done in critical operations and to explain why it is done in a particular way. Using this knowledge, you can then optimize and reengineer operations.

In reengineering, functional business units are divided into process units. This may require redeploying workers in multidisciplinary teams that concentrate on getting the right products and services to the customer just in time. Once process units are developed, then teams can proceduralize the systems and determine the most efficient and effective methods for performing the work.

After processes are reconfigured, you can control and minimize process variation by writing procedures that stress consistency and efficiency. Pro-ceduralization ensures that the little things are done right and are done consis-tently, and consistency and efficiency are essential if you are to control and maintain quality.

Statistical process control is a technique to ensure that process variation is within an acceptable range of variation, or in other words, the variation is consistent around the process target. If process variation goes beyond the acceptable range, the process is stopped and the cause of the unacceptable variation is eliminated. (See Figure 2.1.)

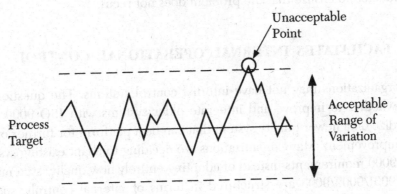

FIGURE 2.1
Process Variation

ENCOURAGES AN INTERNAL FOCUS

Through ISO 9000 implementation, employees understand operations so that they can make them more efficient and effective. The following analogy is from the just-in-time literature, but it applies equally well to ISO 9000. Writing procedures and work instructions focuses attention on internal operations—how things run, why they are running that way, and what can be done to improve them. This attention uncovers the organizational stumbling blocks that impede material flow, cause mistakes, add variation, and deter quality.

By developing, writing, and deploying quality policy development, you will clarify your organization's vision and mission. Quality procedure development details the interaction among functional groups. Work instruction development reveals how work is conducted. With this understanding, you can uncover and solve chronic and systemic problems.

ESTABLISHES PRODUCTION CREDIBILITY

ISO 9001/9002/9003 quality documents were designed primarily for production operations. ISO 9000 registration indicates that a company has the requisite quality systems in place and working effectively. Quality systems demonstrate the supplier has inspection and process controls in place to ensure consistency.

If a discrepancy appears, other quality systems specify that deficient products are to be segregated and identified. Corrective actions are then implemented to remove the symptom and the root cause of the deficiency. Then periodic audits are conducted to ensure that the problem does not recur.

FACILITATES INTERNAL OPERATIONAL CONTROL

Some organizations may not have internal control systems. The question becomes whether to improve and integrate older systems with ISO 9000 or to standardize on a newer quality system that can be a platform for further operational improvement. Many organizations are deciding to adapt existing systems to ISO 9000 requirements instead of adopting entirely new quality systems.

ISO 9001/9002/9003 are structured in terms of internal controls, such as design control and management review. Controls can be thought of as a form of good management practice. Internal operational controls ensure that

- Processes are in control,

- Processes are capable of meeting specifications, and

- Processes are improving.

And if deficiencies should arise, they are root cause corrected so they don't recur. ISO 9000 implementation establishes internal control systems for design, purchasing, and product handling.

ASSISTS EMPLOYEES IN UNDERSTANDING AND IMPROVING OPERATIONS

ISO 9000 implementation encourages employee "buy-in." Employees understand quality policies, procedures, and work instructions and even modify or write work instructions. Why? Because the people who work daily on a process or machine know its intricacies. They also know that work instructions, for example, can be used for training new personnel.

ENCOURAGES SELF-ASSESSMENT

Internal auditing is one of the twenty quality system requirements of ISO 9001. Internal auditing is a major—some say the most important—quality systems requirement.

Internal auditing provides an organization with the following benefits:

- Operations are continuously monitored,

- If deficiencies occur, they are eliminated,

- System problems are uncovered, and

- Chronic problems are discovered and eliminated.

MAINTAINS INTERNAL CONSISTENCY

ISO 9000 encourages a company to identify critical customer requirements and develop procedures to satisfy these requirements. These procedures promote consistent operations to produce consistent products and services. Customers get what they want and expect every time in every product, in every phone call, and in every service.

CONTROLS PROCESSES AND SYSTEMS

ISO 9000 implementation emphasizes proceduralizing operations. Essential quality tasks are made consistent with a goal of minimizing variation in

- Machines,

- Employees,

- Procedures,

- Suppliers, and

- The environment.

MAKES INTERNAL OPERATIONS MORE EFFICIENT AND EFFECTIVE

Many rewards are in ISO 9000 implementation, not necessarily in ISO 9000 registration. ISO 9000 implementation encourages an internal focus to evaluate whether operations are efficient and effective. Specifically, it encourages an organization to ask:

- What are we doing?

- Do our activities add value?

- Can they be done better?

ENSURES THAT PRODUCT DESIGN CHANGES
ARE CONTROLLED

Because rapid product development is essential for survival and product flaws can result in expensive recalls, problems must be corrected during the design stage, not when products are in customers' hands. Design review—a critical ISO 9001 quality system requirement—minimizes design modifications and flaws.

CREATES AN AWARENESS OF THE NEED
FOR TRAINING

Training is another major ISO 9000 quality system requirement. The learning organization is becoming as important as the quality organization. Why? Customers want more products and service options faster, production equipment is becoming more sophisticated, and employees need current skills to use the sophisticated equipment. ISO 9000 implementation encourages that

- Operations are understood, detailed, and documented,

- Employees are accountable for operations, and

- Employees are empowered to control and improve operations.

ENCOURAGES OPERATIONAL PROBLEM SOLVING

Proceduralizing operations reveals opportunities to reengineer and improve operations. Reengineering asks, "Why are we doing this, and how is it adding value?" ISO 9000 implementation asks, "How can we control what we are doing and create consistency?"

CUSTOMER AND SUPPLIER PARTNERING BENEFITS

ISO 9000 are customer and supplier documents. It is notable that the first companies to have registered in the United States are mainly *Fortune 500* sites. Why? Companies with overseas operations are aware of the importance of ISO 9000 registration as a means to ensuring market entry.

The next big growth in registration in the commercial sector will come from large U.S.-registered companies requiring their suppliers to register. In some cases, registration may become the first level of customer and supplier certification required by these companies.

In general, registration will bring about the following customer and supplier partnering benefits. It

- Forms the basis for a common language of quality,

- Ensures a minimum level of quality,

- Facilitates development of seamless operations with suppliers,

- Reduces supplier base,

- Harmonizes commercial and regulated quality specifications,

- Facilitates just-in-time delivery,

- Assists in selecting suppliers,

- Assists in monitoring suppliers, and

- Avoids duplicative quality audits.

FORMS THE BASIS FOR A COMMON LANGUAGE OF QUALITY

What is total quality management (TQM)? There are many models of quality, including the Deming, Juran, Crosby, European Quality Award, Malcolm Baldrige, and organizational development models. Each quality model has its benefits and virtues, but they are all slightly different: they use different vocabularies, emphasize different concepts, and recommend different paths to quality improvement.

ISO 9000 provides globally accepted quality concepts and vocabulary that can be used by global customers and suppliers to communicate and resolve contractual, quality, and delivery differences.

ENSURES A MINIMUM LEVEL OF QUALITY

A total quality management initiative conveys to customers and others that a company is run efficiently and effectively. ISO 9000 registration creates a level playing field of quality suppliers. ISO 9000 registration connotes

- Quality commitment,
- A minimum level of quality, and
- Compatible quality systems.

FACILITATES DEVELOPMENT OF SEAMLESS OPERATIONS WITH SUPPLIERS

Companies are organizing work around processes and systems such as ISO 9000 with a goal of adding value and developing smooth, seamless operations with suppliers. As more work is outsourced to quality suppliers, ISO 9000 brings suppliers closer to customers:

- Internal controls are in place and operating properly,
- Internal controls are documented and maintained, and
- If problems arise, they are fixed and corrected so they don't recur.

REDUCES SUPPLIER BASE

Supplier base is being reduced through customer-supplier certification initiatives. A supplier is rated as a candidate, conditional, or approved, and as a preferred supplier. ISO 9000 registration or implementation is used to satisfy the first or second level of the customer-supplier certification requirement. In other words, to be on the approved bidder's list, suppliers are expected to either be registered to ISO 9001/9002/9003 or have implemented its quality systems. (See Figure 2.2.)

FIGURE 2.2
Example of Customer-Supplier Certification

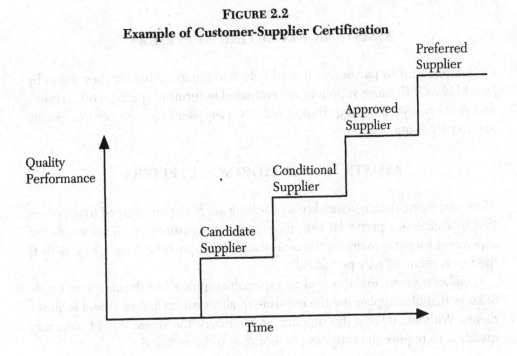

HARMONIZES COMMERCIAL AND REGULATED QUALITY SPECIFICATIONS

Military and regulated-industry quality systems are similar because they are based on the same parent specification—MIL-Q 9858A. These specifications are documentation intensive. Commercial customer-supplier specifications diverged from MIL-Q and became customer and prevention driven. ISO 9000 adoption by all sectors—the military, regulated, and commercial—will standardize quality terms, concepts, and implementation.

FACILITATES JUST-IN-TIME DELIVERY

Customers want the right material delivered just in time, at the proper count, and in the right sequence to the right location. Suppliers implementing ISO 9000 quality systems have storage, handling, and delivery quality systems in place to facilitate the smooth and quick transfer of products. Handling, storage, and delivery quality systems ensure that products are also free from defects. If delivery problems do occur, they are resolved quickly.

ASSISTS IN SELECTING SUPPLIERS

Customers want to partner with world-class suppliers. What do they mean by "world class"? Because suppliers are evaluated in terms of quality, cost, service, and delivery, ISO 9000 registration reflects a supplier's commitment to quality and to partnering.

ASSISTS IN MONITORING SUPPLIERS

More and more, design, assembly, and testing are being outsourced to suppliers that specialize in a particular test, inspection, or measurement. This avoids the expense of having to maintain the expertise and equipment in house, especially if the test is required only periodically.

It makes sense to send the work to a specialty supplier, but the customer needs to know that the supplier has the requisite quality systems and can meet requirements. Without auditing the supplier or laboratory, the surest way of obtaining quality is to require the supplier or laboratory to be certified.

AVOIDS DUPLICATIVE QUALITY AUDITS

In the regulated, commercial, and military sectors, customer and supplier audits are conducted yearly or even more frequently. These quality audits often assess the same international, national, or industry standards. They are duplicative and costly.

As regulatory authorities, the military, and commercial industry sectors adopt ISO 9000, one audit of any supplier should satisfy the requirements of all customers. A customer would need only to check a ISO 9000 supplier registry to determine a supplier's status.

ISO 9000 REGISTRATION CHALLENGES

ISO 9000 registration and implementation are not without challenges. They require time, money, personnel, and other resources. In addition to gathering these resources, any organization considering ISO 9000 needs to understand, discuss, and evaluate the following constraints and challenges to ISO 9000 registration:

- Increased government involvement,
- Political confusion about the future of registration activities,
- Overcertification,
- Adding cost, not value,
- Credibility loss,
- No guarantee of customer satisfaction or product quality,
- Registration dismissal by some companies,
- Appearance of registrar conflicts of interest,
- Variation in auditor quality,
- Differences in interpreting ISO 9000 standards,
- Documentation that does not satisfy customers,
- Hindering organizational creativity and innovation,
- Lack of understanding of purposes and goals of conformity assessment,
- No emphasis on continuous improvement, and
- Overpromise and underdelivery by consultants.

INCREASED GOVERNMENT INVOLVEMENT

Free trade will increase as countries continue removing tariff and other types of economic barriers. But national governments also probably will become more involved in regulating the accreditation process and establishing national certification structures in their countries. Governments also will accelerate the negotiating of mutual recognition agreements for certifying health, safety, and environmental products. In time, quality systems registration in Portugal, Bangladesh, and the United States should be similar.

POLITICAL CONFUSION ABOUT THE FUTURE OF REGISTRATION ACTIVITIES

ISO 9000 accreditation and registration in the United States is largely self-regulating, but the U.S. government has proposed becoming active throughout the process—from establishing mutual recognition agreements among countries to certifying accreditors, certifying registrars, and evaluating quality auditors. Currently, there is widespread agreement that the government should become involved only in nation-to-nation agreements and that everything else should be voluntary and left to the marketplace. Presently, certification in the United States is largely a private effort. However, the U.S. government will become more active as North American trade picks up.

OVERCERTIFICATION

ISO 9000 registration is only the first certification step. The European and Pacific Rim nations regulate their citizens' lives more than the United States does. As world trade increases and product components come from many countries, product certificates and quality system registrations will increase. A product could carry environmental, safety, ISO 9000 registration, and other types of labels. Certification shouldn't become a bureaucratic exercise but should continue to add market value.

ADDING COST, NOT VALUE

ISO 9000 registration in the United States is not increasing as quickly as some observers initially believed it would. Companies are asking, "What value does this add to my organization?" Until this question can be answered to the satisfaction of everyone in your organization, ISO 9000 registration should not be pursued. ISO 9000 implementation, however—using ISO 9000 documents to become more efficient and effective—can still be pursued.

CREDIBILITY LOSS

If ISO 9000 auditors conduct bad audits and registrars lower their quality, ISO 9000 registration in the United States and throughout the world will lose its credibility. The entire structure of recognizing audit results is based on credibility and trust, and trust will evaporate without self-control and self-regulation among registrars. For example, if registrars compete through lowering costs, and companies begin to shop registrars to obtain the lowest price, the quality of the audits could be lowered.

NO GUARANTEE OF CUSTOMER SATISFACTION OR PRODUCT QUALITY

Registrars certify that ISO 9001/9002/9003 quality systems exist and operate properly. However, even the best systems, processes, and internal controls will not guarantee complete customer satisfaction, product quality, safety, or compliance with other regulatory requirements. The registrar's auditors conduct the initial audit and subsequent surveillance audits to ensure that company policies reflect ISO 9000 requirements, that quality procedures are implemented complying with company policies, and that work instructions specify how procedures are followed. The auditors during the initial and surveillance audits sample only some procedures and work instructions to ensure conformity with the intent of the particular ISO 9000 requirement.

REGISTRATION DISMISSAL BY SOME COMPANIES

Some companies have dismissed ISO 9000 as nothing more than another "flavor of the month" public relations gimmick. Small companies, in particular, may see only the high cost of registration. Even the smallest company, however, should pay attention to ISO 9000 developments because customers within their industry sector may expect suppliers to become registered.

A small supplier may find itself blindsided unless it is prepared. A customer may expect it to become registered within six months, but without the quality systems or the documentation to support quality systems, the supplier may lose business. It's smarter to understand and preempt industry developments and start implementing at least modest quality systems early on.

APPEARANCE OF REGISTRAR CONFLICTS OF INTEREST

Many registrars currently supply consulting and other advisory services. An appearance of a conflict of interest may arise if the same people conducting the quality systems audits also provide consulting on how to become registered.

VARIATION IN AUDITOR QUALITY

Quality auditing is largely a new discipline with a minimum number of entry requirements. This creates the possibility that unqualified people are conducting quality system audits of operations with which they are not familiar. Registrars are trying to remedy this deficiency by carefully screening and training their auditors.

DIFFERENCES IN INTERPRETING ISO 9000 STANDARDS

ISO 9000 family series of documents is a one-size-fits-all set of standards that can be used in many different types of organizations from manufacturing to health care. However, ISO 9000 auditors may have to interpret how internal process-specific documents satisfy ISO 9000 requirements.

DOCUMENTATION THAT DOES NOT SATISFY CUSTOMERS

ISO 9000 is documentation intensive, but it does not address internal or external customer satisfaction. Quality documents don't satisfy customers: they simply reflect the state of the business.

HINDERING ORGANIZATIONAL CREATIVITY AND INNOVATION

Too much documentation and proceduralization can stifle creativity and innovation. Employees may feel they have to do their jobs in a specific manner, especially if procedures and work instructions are imposed on them from above. This can be resolved by having the people who actually perform work assist in developing work instructions so they reflect how work is actually done.

LACK OF UNDERSTANDING OF PURPOSES AND GOALS OF CONFORMITY ASSESSMENT

Conformity assessment is the overall term for ensuring that products, laboratories, and quality systems comply with customer requirements. Conformity assessment may include an ISO 9000 audit, product testing, or laboratory assessment. Different products and industries emphasize or require different conformity assessment. A company producing regulated products needs to understand industry, customer, and other requirements.

NO EMPHASIS ON CONTINUOUS IMPROVEMENT

ISO 9000 is rewritten every five years. Customer service, benchmarking, continuous improvement, quality measurement, and other state-of-the-art topics are not covered in the present ISO 9001/9002/9003 documents. Future revisions will probably incorporate these topics.

OVERPROMISE AND UNDERDELIVERY BY CONSULTANTS

Misinterpretation and misinformation surround ISO 9000 registration. Whose fault is this? In some cases, consultants are overpromising. In the United States, accreditation and registration are still evolving. As with any important business decision, potential registrants should ask a lot of questions. The more you know, the easier registration will be.

In the next Step we discuss how to secure management commitment which is absolutely critical to successful ISO 9000 registration.

STEP 3

SECURE MANAGEMENT COMMITMENT

Key Steps
• Form a quality council.
• Secure management's support as the sponsor of change and champion of the ISO 9000 initiative.
• Eliminate the "flavor-of-the-month" cynicism.
• Introduce the ISO 9000 purposes, goals, and benefits to all employees.
• Couple ISO 9000 implementation with other initiatives such as learning or organizational change.
• Anticipate and plan for internal resistance.
• Intervene at crisis or resistance points.
• Develop and instill organizational commitment.
• Include first-level supervisors and representatives of middle management on the quality council.

Top management provides the impetus to ISO 9000 registration, and ISO 9000 registration requires its continuing active commitment throughout the process. ISO 9000 implementation or registration requires people, money, and other resources to initiate. During the process, top management needs to communicate, explain, convince, and use other means to involve the organization.

MANAGEMENT ROLES AND FUNCTIONS: THE QUALITY COUNCIL

Management must actively commit to and participate throughout the registration project. It is easy for management to endorse the concept of the registration project and then delegate it to others. When the first major problem or conflict arises, however, that initial enthusiasm may wear thin as costs mount and registration time is prolonged. The entire organization must understand the short- and long-term benefits of implementation and registration, of course, but the true success of the effort depends on the perceptions, attitudes, and expectations of the people who create and use the quality systems on a day-to-day basis.

Where should the authorization for ISO 9000 registration come from? Authorization for registering the entire organization comes from the executive steering committee. If only one site is being registered, then the site general manager can authorize the registration.

As a first step, management may either authorize a team to research the benefits and challenges of ISO 9000 implementation or authorize a pilot ISO 9000 implementation at one or two sites. Each site then would form its own team to coordinate the process, communicate with the registrar, and write procedures.

Depending on the size of the organization and the number of sites to be registered, an ISO 9000 quality council may be formed to acquire information, make decisions, and coordinate efforts dealing with the ISO 9000 registration initiative. The council also may authorize the ISO 9000 registration effort.

The council is composed of senior and business unit operations management and other senior organizational stakeholders who can champion, coach, and assist the registration process. The council may empower different ISO 9000 registration teams, provide coordination, supply resources, and communicate the importance of the initiative.

The council should be formed of business unit operations management and functional management and not simply quality department management. This is an important distinction. ISO 9000 quality systems direction and implementation are organization-wide responsibilities, and quality departments usually don't have such authority or perspective. More often, quality implementation rests with operating management, which invests the council with four important roles:

- Key customer and supplier interface,

- Change agent,

- Sponsor, and

- Champion.

What Does Management Do?

Top management drives ISO 9000 registration and its maintenance and actively supports the ISO 9000 registration initiative by

- Championing and sponsoring the ISO 9000 initiative,

- Promoting the benefits of ISO 9000 registration,

- Defining expectations, needs, and requirements clearly,

- Allocating resources,

- Responding to requests quickly,

- Facilitating internal and external ISO 9000 coordination,

- Providing delegation,

- Providing feedback,

- Supplying advice and support,

- Providing training,

- Resolving conflicts, and

- Intervening if necessary.

KEY CUSTOMER AND SUPPLIER INTERFACE

A customer may require registration as a condition of doing business, of being on the approved bidder's list, or of passing the first hurdle in the customer and supplier certification effort. The customer's purchasing department is usually the contact point for the supplier. The customer may ask to be kept notified of the registration progress, or the supplier can assign a senior executive to serve as the customer-supplier interface throughout the registration process. The senior executive communicates and serves as the contact for reporting problems, correcting problems, or reporting progress.

CHANGE AGENT

What was acceptable yesterday is often not acceptable today. Competitive pressures are forcing changes at dizzying speed. Concepts like customer responsiveness, high-performance teams, and high-velocity performance are being introduced, and processes are being reengineered and proceduralized. Process constraints are being eliminated, and value is being added in each activity.

ISO 9000 registration and implementation are used as a mechanism for creating organizational change, redesigning operations, proceduralizing, developing self-managed teams, and establishing and documenting quality systems.

SPONSOR

A member of the council often becomes the executive sponsor of the ISO 9000 registration. The sponsor is visible evidence of top management's commitment to ISO 9000 implementation or registration. The sponsor is also the council's eyes, ears, and hands during the registration effort and provides the link between top management and the ISO 9000 implementation team.

A common problem that arises once registration effort is underway is that upper management divorces itself from the ISO 9000 implementation. Too much is delegated to the team or untrained subordinates. There may be misdirection or inaction because the purpose or direction of the activities is not clearly understood. When this happens, the sponsor advises the team on how to regain its focus.

CHAMPION

Another critical role played by management in the registration process is the role of ISO 9000 champion. The champion may sit on the quality council, report to the council, or be the ISO 9000 team leader. The sponsor and the champion may be the same person and assume both roles. The champion attends ISO 9000 team meetings, serves as cheerleader, supplies training, is a problem solver, acquires resources, is involved in planning, resolves conflicts, and reports progress.

The champion may also be the ISO 9000 team leader, but day-to-day management of the ISO 9000 project and cheerleading sometimes can conflict. The ISO 9000 team leader may appear to be promoting his or her importance instead of communicating the registration benefits. For this reason, the two functions are often separated.

Team conflicts and problems can be resolved within the ISO 9000 registration team. The team may find it more difficult to resolve conflicts across organizational lines—for example, problems with business units or external departments whose cooperation is required. The sponsor or champion should have the perspective as well as the authority to resolve these problems.

Is there a rule of thumb that can be used to determine what problems the champion or sponsor should be consulted on? No. As a general rule, whenever a problem affects registration budgets, time constraints, or performance, then the champion may have to be consulted. However, the champion or sponsor should not make tactical or technical decisions; these are the responsibility of the ISO 9000 team. The sponsor or the champion shouldn't meddle or micromanage the

---

Do You Need to Establish a Quality Council?

Should every organization form a council? No. But every organization should have a group, team, or individual keenly aware of the marketplace and its competitive pressures that can sense the need for quality, delivery, technology, service, or cost or profit opportunities. Sometimes the opportunities are quality related, and sometimes they deal with pricing issues.

How large should the council be? The council can vary in size and responsibilities. In a small company of less than 200 employees located in only several sites, the council could be the main ISO 9000 registration team. In a larger company with multiple business units and multiple sites, the council is the umbrella organization for facilitating multiple registrations. This council establishes and empowers other site teams to pursue registrations at sites or to write procedures. For example, at a plant that supplies natural gas products that are regulated in Europe, the plant manager may believe that registration soon will be required and would help position its products with customers. Instead of hiring consultants, the plant manager can consult with the corporate council, which can provide monies, consulting, or training to facilitate the process.

Management Success Tips

False starts, mistakes, and errors will be encountered during the ISO 9000 implementation and registration process. The entire effort involves learning new quality technologies and perhaps adapting existing operations. Here are some tips for success:

- *Create realistic expectations.* Registration is not a panacea for internal problems, for instant competitiveness, for lowering costs, or for creating a world-class total quality program. Registration is the first step in a long journey of continuous improvement. Management, employees, and other stakeholders may see registration as much more than it is and build unrealistic expectations.

- *Think small and work in increments.* ISO 9000 registration is a doable project. Think small and work in increments. For a large company with multiple plants in many locations, pilot your effort in one or two locations first. The lessons learned from this effort can be transferred to other locations.

- *Ensure that a senior manager actively and visibly champions the registration effort.* If senior management support is unclear, then the successful completion of the project is unclear. This results in an uneasy feeling among the ISO 9000 registration team members as well as the organization.

---

registration process; this disempowers the team and may be perceived as an unwanted intrusion, which eventually may lead to a breakdown in trust. If necessary, the team should inform the sponsor that it appreciates that top management trusts the team members to get the job done. The sponsor usually gets the message that micromanagement will disrupt the registration process and will step aside, allowing the team to develop its own plan, timeline, and accountabilities.

ELIMINATING THE FLAVOR OF THE MONTH

ISO 9000 quality initiatives sometimes stall. The reasons may vary: ISO 9000 implementation may be perceived as "the flavor of the month" program, or an organization may have many simultaneous projects on its plate or may reject the imposition of the ISO 9000 graft, or people may not have been trained or provided with adequate resources.

Properly communicated, ISO 9000 implementation can be used as a means to transform an organization into a high-powered organization of highly productive, self-managed teams. Members of the self-managed teams are empowered to plan and execute day-to-day work decisions and operations with little or no supervision.

DANGERS OF IMPOSING ISO 9000 QUALITY
SYSTEMS AND REGISTRATION

ISO 9000 registration should not be imposed on the organization. There needs to be organizational consensus about its value. Nevertheless, ISO 9000 registration effort can be difficult for line business units, plants, and functional departments. It can result in

- Reprioritizing internal projects because of the registration mandate,

- Unplanned loss of personnel to ISO 9000 team participation,

- Additional variation in the process,

- Fewer personnel on the line to solve problems,

- Limited operational resources,

- Additional overhead costs because of required ISO 9000 activities, and

- Scheduling problems resulting from requiring personnel to write procedures.

Business unit, line, or functional management may perceive ISO 9000 implementation as still another special project or initiative required of them in addition to their responsibilities for daily operations. Line management may believe it can't both satisfy management's requirements for ISO 9000 registration as well as operate the plant on a daily basis to provide consistent quality and to reduce costs. Factory floor employees or receptionists already are fully occupied with their responsibilities to monitor machinery and answer phones.

Faced with this type of resistance, top management may well require participation from line groups and mandate ISO 9000 team participation. This simply won't work. Management needs to avoid being seen as trying to indoctrinate employees into the language and systems of ISO 9000.

ISO 9000 registration has to be seen and felt by the organization as one of the bases of the corporation's marketplace or operational strategy. For example, a customer that produces a regulated product may require ISO 9000 compliance. If customer expectations are firmly explained and understood by most employees—and most companies have requirements that meet or exceed customer expectations—the foundation has been set for the ISO 9000 implementation.

People become wary of change imposed on them and may lose their motivation if ISO 9000 tasks are mandated from above. During this unsettling period when employees carry out their normal day-to-day tasks as well as implement ISO 9000 registration, the benefits and rewards coming from ISO 9000 implementation may not resonate with the hourly or exempt worker. Customer satisfaction, competitiveness, regulatory compliance, and performance enhancement are benefits of ISO 9000 implementation that can be communicated so that average employees can feel that ISO 9000 implementation is an empowering mechanism.

MANAGING THE CULTURAL CHANGE

The technical issues of registration are fairly straightforward. The organizational issues, however, are more challenging. Management must actively support the effort. Practices may have to change. Teams must be formed. Resistance must be dealt with. Inertia throughout the project must be overcome. High expectations of instant results have to be dealt with.

ISO 9000 implementation should be done in a structured and systematic manner reflecting the culture of the organization. ISO 9000 and other quality management techniques cannot be imposed unilaterally on an organization. The organization may well reject the effort. Management also cannot develop the quality manual and documentation and impose it on the organization and then wonder why quality systems don't function properly. ISO 9000 works well when integrated slowly into the business and when it has an opportunity to evolve. Top management promotes registration, employees realize its value, and documentation flows out of the process. The purpose of ISO 9000 registration or implementation should first be explained and understood by all employees, and then gradually the culture of the organization should adapt to ISO 9000 principles.

The purpose of registration can be explained in either a negative or positive manner. Management can explain that if the company doesn't respond to customer needs, it will win fewer contracts and need fewer workers to fulfill those contracts. A more positive approach is to present ISO 9000 as a tool that is being used to improve the quality of work life. Quality systems reduce process variation, increase the quality of end-products, reduce rework, and thereby increase quality of work life. (See Figure 3.1.)

INTERNAL RESISTANCE

ISO 9000 implementation is about people. Systems may be adopted, others may be adapted to ISO 9000 requirements, and other changes may be instituted. People will resist change unless they understand the reasons for it. Within the technical system—the quality systems, processes, and products and the physical environment—the human factors involve the nature of the organization, culture, management styles, psychological skills, and education levels. If people resist or can't absorb new ideas, ISO 9000 systems may have to be implemented slowly. In some cases, quality system proceduralization may not fit the environment. In a

FIGURE 3.1
Process Improvement Through Reducing Variation

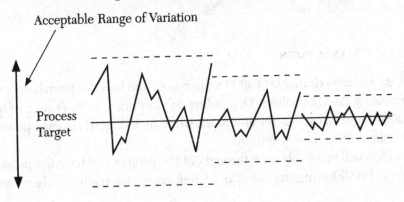

research and development lab, for example, scientists and engineers may resist proceduralization and paperwork.

How is this resistance relieved? People will implement systems only if they see the benefits and value to them personally. ISO 9000 implementation becomes regimentation if people are pushed. ISO 9000 systems should be matched as much as possible to the people and to their work environment.

Signs of Impending Problems

ISO 9000 registration can be secured by any organization. The challenge is to achieve registration as simply as possible. The following are signs of impending problems:

- Insufficient resources,

- Lack of interest,

- Lack of cooperation,

- Unclear objectives,

- Changing priorities,

- Conflicting messages,

- Poor direction from management,

- Lack of management support,

- No team cooperation and coordination,

- No funding, and

- Internal resistance.

CONFLICT MANAGEMENT

Conflicts will arise during ISO 9000 registration, and how the team handles them determines success or failure. Depending on your organization's state of quality, ISO 9000 registration may require much work, including developing procedures and implementing quality systems.

Conflicts will inevitably arise throughout the project and have the potential to derail the ISO 9000 registration effort. Conflicts among team members can delay a project's schedule and can ruin a team's morale. An authoritarian style of project management—"My way or the highway" style of management—also destroys morale. Conflicts can destroy the effectiveness of the team, hinder communication, and minimize technical performance. The results are the same—possible schedule slippage or stoppage. If anticipated, conflict can be used creatively to create a sense of urgency and direction to ISO 9000 registration. Authoritarian managers can be trained in team- and performance-based management.

Because most ISO 9000 team members have operational, design, or maintenance jobs requiring full-time involvement, they may perceive ISO 9000 registration as just another project and place ISO 9000 registration at the bottom of their work priorities. Again, it's up to top management to link registration to process improvement, customer satisfaction, quality of work life, and profitability.

INSTILLING ORGANIZATIONAL COMMITMENT

ISO 9000 registration or implementation depends on the active commitment of senior management and the day-to-day commitment of departmental and line management. Since quality is integral to all operations, line management is responsible for implementing and maintaining the quality systems called for in ISO 9001/9002/9003. By extension, self-managed line teams are responsible for day-to-day success and performance of the quality systems.

MIDDLE-MANAGEMENT COMMITMENT AND SUPPORT

Middle managers are often responsible for the implementation of specific quality system requirements. Purchasing managers, for example, are responsible for implementing the customer supplier product and purchasing quality system requirements.

Implementing ISO 9000 quality systems may require work processes to be changed, and change is threatening to disappearing middle management. Traditionally, middle management supervised day-to-day operations, maintained budgets, planned projects, delegated work, and reported progress to top management. With the advent of new sociotechnical organizational styles, self-directed work teams are accountable and have authority for their own work. Senior management can tap into computers to determine progress, performance, and costs without the help of middle management.

This is a major change for line supervisors and middle managers. With the flattening of organizations, however, the middle managers who remain also find that their control and responsibility are much broader than before. Line supervisors may become trainers, auditors, coaches, or facilitators in this team atmosphere.

In this environment, middle managers and supervisors must develop new skills. Traditional authoritarian styles of management simply don't work as well and have to be replaced. Middle managers need to communicate the new organizational values to empower and coach employees to work with these teams.

Tips for Involving Middle Management

Here are some tips for involving middle management in the ISO 9000 registration effort:

- Require functional or area management to appoint a representative to the ISO 9000 team.

- Invite functional management to explain the importance and value of ISO 9000 registration to their organization.

- Ask senior management to hold area or functional management accountable for ISO 9000 implementation.

- Encourage functional or area management to empower teams to implement the quality system directives.

- Invite functional or area management to encourage teams to go beyond the system control requirements spelled out in ISO 9000 by pursuing process improvements and breakthroughs.

- Acknowledge and reward teams for ISO 9000 performance.

FIRST-LEVEL SUPERVISION

As middle management continues to disappear, an important link to successful ISO 9000 implementation is the first-level supervisor. Often this person originally was assigned to rein in the front-line troops—specifically, to discipline, plan, monitor, and punish the people performing the work. Today, however, the first-line supervisor must perform the functions of middle management. As work teams take over line supervision functions, the line supervisor becomes a coach, mentor, problem solver, facilitator, trainer, and assistant to the front-line work teams. By creating a work atmosphere where the teams are motivated and provided with the resources to manage their efforts, the first-line supervisor can recognize and reward ISO 9000 commitment, motivation, innovation, and improvement.

STEP 4

PLAN FOR ISO 9000 REGISTRATION

Key Steps
• Define your ISO 9000 vision, mission, goals, and objectives.
• Develop your ISO 9000 strategic and tactical plans.
• Avert ISO 9000 expectation creep.
• Focus on the doable and the measurable.
• Plan, plan, plan for ISO 9000 registration and implementation.
• Integrate ISO 9000 requirements and systems into existing operations.
• Coordinate with operational and functional management.

Sometimes, ISO 9000 registration is pursued for reasons and motives not clearly evident to all employees. It may be that registration or implementation takes longer or is more expensive than anticipated. Halfway through the process, the ISO 9000 rationale may be questioned. When there is a shift in direction, registration may be put on the back burner.

How should these challenges be solved? ISO 9000 registration should be pursued as an operational plan tied to your organization's strategic plan. The more closely ISO 9000 registration and maintenance are related to the overall goals of your organization, the better your chances of success. Only senior management can convey the importance of registration, and it needs to do so by actively delivering messages about the real benefits that will accrue from registration. Only then will employees understand the purpose and importance of the registration.

Any questions about the intended results and benefits of the project should be clarified early in the registration process. The complexity of the plan will vary depending on the size of the organization, but the plan should be understandable and doable. The plan needs to be accessible because work area members will be implementing the quality systems, writing quality documentation, conducting training, and conducting preliminary assessment.

It's easy for expectations to outrun initial requirements and, indeed, to outrun the entire ISO 9000 registration effort. To avoid this "expectation creep," senior management must ensure that requirements and expectations are congruent throughout the registration effort and that initial requirements for ISO 9000 registration are spelled out early in the project. If management wants it done faster, with fewer people, or with fewer resources than is reasonable, it ultimately may be unhappy with registration performance.

The first step in establishing goals and requirements for the registration process is to identify and involve all the stakeholders of the registration effort. The stakeholder is anyone or any group having a stake in the outcome of the registration project: customers, suppliers, management, government agencies, or other interested parties may be stakeholders. By identifying these groups and clarifying their concerns, requirements, and expectations, you will be better prepared to write your mission and objective statements. Draft these statements to define the requirements of success of the project in doable and measurable terms, and you will be well on the way to a successful ISO 9000 registration. In the next section, we discuss registration strategies for large and small organizations.

WHAT SITES SHOULD BE REGISTERED FIRST?

Once you're aware of the strategic benefits of pursuing registration, the next question to ask is, "What should be registered?"

Registration is usually done by site. There are no hard and fast rules for determining what constitutes a registrable site, but it's critical that you discuss your various site options with the registrar.

In a site registration, one quality manual is used to audit the quality systems and operations at an individual site. Because many companies have multiple sites often organized along product lines, locations, or some other criteria, each site producing different products must have its own registration certificate and be audited individually.

There are several variations to this rule. If a company has one main location and several distribution centers and sales offices, then the main office and satellite centers would be audited and placed on the same certificate.

Even many small businesses of less than 200 employees have multiple sites. The basic question is whether all sites have similar processes producing similar products using the same procedures. If the answer is yes, then one registration certificate can cover all sites.

REGISTRATION STRATEGIES

Organizations are following several approaches to ISO 9000 registration:

- Registering all business units, plants, and sites,

- Registering selected sites depending on customer, competitive, or regulatory requirements,

- Registering depending on the needs of individual operational managers, or

- Registering a pilot site.

REGISTERING ALL BUSINESS UNITS, PLANTS, AND SITES

Some companies are registering all their business sites and plants. Why? A company may realize that ISO 9000 isn't fading away, may understand its benefits, and may want to position itself proactively in the marketplace by advertising that all plants are registered. Regulated and commercial product manufacturers also are realizing that sooner or later registration may be required. So companies are registering in anticipation of needing to harmonize customer and supplier quality requirements to ISO 9001/9002/9003. Many companies already have quality systems in place and realize that registration is a business expense that can be easily recaptured.

REGISTERING SELECTED SITES DEPENDING ON CUSTOMER, COMPETITIVE, OR REGULATORY REQUIREMENTS

Some companies are registering only sites that produce regulated systems or that need to conform to a customer requirement. The company may consider that, in general, registration is expensive, disruptive to operations, or not value adding.

REGISTERING DEPENDING ON THE NEEDS OF INDIVIDUAL OPERATIONAL MANAGERS

A large organization may have five or more different product lines. In this case, each business unit manager will look at and analyze the benefits of registration based on customer requirements, market conditions, and other factors. This decision will be entirely independent of other business units or what the corporation may want.

REGISTERING A PILOT SITE

One method for developing organization-wide implementation in a large organization is to start a pilot at one site. The pilot becomes the dry run for the entire organization or other sites. Lessons learned in the pilot are used at other sites so that mistakes are not repeated. The pilot is done first, and then the rest of the organizational sites are done concurrently.

REGISTRATION OF LARGE AND SMALL ORGANIZATIONS

Since many types of organizations may be pursuing ISO 9000 registration, we are examining ISO 9000 registration from a general perspective. Often registration, whether in a large or small organization, follows the same process. Why? Most large organizations consist of stand-alone profit centers that are often divisions, business units, departments, or plants. A large organization often has many sites and pursues registration on a site-by-site basis.

LARGE ORGANIZATION REGISTRATION

Still, the registration plan for large, multisite organizations is different than for smaller organizations. The large organization has staff and resources often unavailable to a small organization that provide real advantages when pursuing registration. A large organization has the following registration advantages:

- Time to register is often shorter from six months to a year.
- Communications are easier among team members.
- Electronic quality documentation is generated.
- Cooperation throughout the organization may be higher.
- Process restructuring is easier.
- Gap analysis and documentation writing is easier.
- More resources may be invested in the project.
- Quality systems and processes already exist.
- The training function is already well accepted.

SMALL ORGANIZATION REGISTRATION

Implementation or registration in a small organization has the following challenges:

- The team leader and members have multiple duties—functional responsibilities as well as team responsibilities.
- The team leader and members may work on multiple teams.
- Staff in a small organization is limited, so team members may have to do their own typing and photocopying.
- Team members may have to develop all the quality documentation.
- Money and other resources are tight.
- There are few or no quality controls or systems in place.
- The owner or other stakeholders in a small business may interfere or intervene in the project.

- The ISO 9000 project team may well report to the owner or to the top person in a small business.

- Planning and preparation for the audit may be weak.

- Training does not exist.

- Internal resistance to change may be high.

In the next section, we discuss the critical elements of developing a registration plan.

THE ACTION PLAN

How should ISO 9000 registration be pursued in terms of your organization?

THREE MODELS

The following are several descriptive models that have been implemented:

- Force fit,

- Shoehorn, and

- Integration.

FORCE FIT

In force fit implementation, someone within the organization, often the CEO, mandates that registration will be pursued—usually because a customer demands it quickly. The owner or CEO makes a unilateral decision that registration is necessary for the organization. Stakeholders are not consulted. It just will be done. In this scenario, external consultants often are retained to force feed employees with ISO 9000 principles, systems, and documentation. Operations are disrupted. Organizational culture may be changed. This is a difficult process, even in the best of times.

SHOEHORN

Shoehorn implementation is similar to a force fit. ISO 9000 quality systems are adapted to the organization as well as possible. Overlapping or parallel systems of control may be developed. For example, there may be overlapping operational procedures, commercial quality systems, and ISO 9000-based quality systems. This redundancy can become a documentation nightmare if each customer has its own requirements that are met with different quality and operational systems.

INTEGRATION

ISO 9000 concepts, techniques, and systems are broad and can be integrated into almost any system or organization. In shoehorning, parallel systems are established. With integration, existing systems are maintained, and ISO 9000 quality systems are fit around the existing structure. As much as possible, existing methods, procedures, training, resource flows, and environment are kept the same.

TECHNICAL PLANNING REQUIREMENTS

Although we are following one path to ISO 9000 registration, there are other options to secure ISO 9000 registration. It is important that ISO 9000 registration fits your organization. Some steps may be less important or useful than others. Some steps may not be included in this book. This book can serve as a tool or template for your registration effort.

The secret to a successful ISO 9000 registration is careful planning. In general, ISO 9000 project planning involves identifying and acquiring resources to achieve the desired goal—in this case, ISO 9000 registration.

The first objective in developing the plan is to understand why registration is being pursued. If this is understood, then timelines, resource allocations, priorities, schedules, and other project requirements will be available when needed.

The plan details in a broad manner how the team will achieve its registration objectives. It doesn't have to be a complex document. The plan should identify the steps for becoming ISO 9000 registered. You need to avoid falling into the trap of developing a complex document that pinpoints who does what at every step in the proper sequence. People become bogged down by excessive planning, and the registration effort will stall.

Planning Checklist

The following is a list of items to consider in creating your ISO 9000 planning checklist:

- Evaluate alternatives to registration, including product testing, second-party auditing, and so on.

- Evaluate competitive advantages.

- Evaluate regulatory pressures.

- Evaluate marketing and promotional potentials.

- Evaluate cost effectiveness.

- Evaluate internal capabilities.

- Assess management support.

- Quantify weaknesses, disadvantages, and risks.

- Evaluate time, cost, performance, and resource requirements.

- Prepare preliminary cost evaluations.

- Prepare an initial plan.

- Develop project specifications.

- Prepare a milestone schedule.

- Break down work requirements.

- Allocate resources.

- Assess risks.

- Select team members.

- Determine the start and finish dates.

- Determine the preassessment date.

- Select a registrar.

When drafting your plan, focus on these basic questions:

- What is the objective of ISO 9000 registration?

- Who is responsible for registration and is authorized to implement it?

- What are the major milestones in the plan?

- When is it going to start?

- Why is registration being pursued?

- What resources are required?

- How is registration being pursued?

- What location will be registered?

How long does it take to become ISO 9001 registered? It depends on:

- Size of organization,

- Management commitment,

- State of quality system,

- Quality documentation.

Figure 4.1 illustrates a registration timeline for a small organization to achieve ISO 9001. It should be stressed that depending on the above factors, registration steps and timelines can change.

FIGURE 4.1
ISO 9000 Registration Process

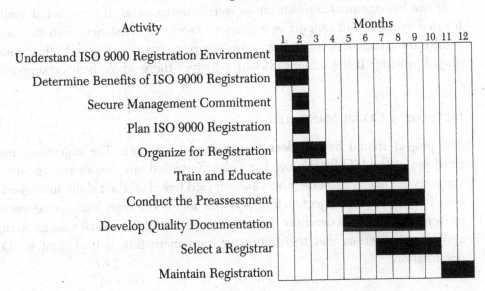

Activity	Months
	1 2 3 4 5 6 7 8 9 10 11 12
Understand ISO 9000 Registration Environment	
Determine Benefits of ISO 9000 Registration	
Secure Management Commitment	
Plan ISO 9000 Registration	
Organize for Registration	
Train and Educate	
Conduct the Preassessment	
Develop Quality Documentation	
Select a Registrar	
Maintain Registration	

ORGANIZATIONAL PLANNING REQUIREMENTS

ISO 9000 registration involves organizational planning as much as establishing technical systems. Consider the following organizational elements when developing a plan:

- Air conflicting views.

- Develop a clear mandate.

- Understand your planning goals and commitments.

- Coordinate with functional units.

- Avoid the quick-fix syndrome.

- Estimate time requirements.

- Secure internal support.

AIR CONFLICTING VIEWS

At this point, there should be a go or no-go decision. If there is still some doubt within the organization about the value of registration, then conflicting points of view should be aired, understood, and resolved. Otherwise, these conflicts may deter implementation or registration.

Senior management conflicts are especially detrimental. If there is only half-hearted management support or middle-management resistance, then stop and resolve the issues. Ask yourself why are you pursuing registration? What value does it provide? If the value is evident, why isn't there whole-hearted support?

DEVELOP A CLEAR MANDATE

The project should have a clear organizational mandate. The objectives and timelines of the ISO 9000 project are clearly spelled out. Senior management supports the team. Team members are selected based on their skills and experience to carry out the project on time and on budget. The team leader, champion, or facilitator is chosen carefully. There is management, functional management, and team consensus that registration or implementation is important to the organization.

UNDERSTAND YOUR PLANNING GOALS AND COMMITMENTS

Preparing for ISO 9000 registration is the major time-, resource-, and labor-consuming activity in ISO 9000 registration. Preparation may consume up to 90 or more percent of the total direct labor hours in the registration project before the auditor actually visits a facility, and for fairly straightforward reasons. Internal assessments have to be conducted, and policies, procedures, and work instructions have to be written. These are very resource- and time-consuming activities.

COORDINATE WITH FUNCTIONAL UNITS

The ISO 9000 team will be working with functional units to develop procedures. Functional units should know what is involved with registration, including the functional personnel required to develop and write procedure and work instructions. The goal is to avoid straining or destabilizing operations.

The ISO 9000 team or the ISO 9000 coordinator in a small registration does not have the resources to develop all the procedures. She or he must communicate with the functional managers so that they are aware of the potential for schedule, resource, and work changes in their departments. Changes also can affect downstream and upstream departments as well, so they also should be kept informed.

AVOID THE QUICK-FIX SYNDROME

Senior management may perceive registration as another short-term project or as a quick fix for a customer registration request. Once it's accomplished, the organization can move forward with other projects. Registration, however, is an ongoing process of maintenance and continuous improvement. Surveillance audits occur every six months, and full audits every three years. The standards are rewritten every four to five years. The challenge for the organization is to maintain interest throughout the registration process and beyond.

ESTIMATE TIME REQUIREMENTS

Develop a realistic estimate of the amount of time registration takes. The length of time that registration takes depends on many variables, including the following:

- Customer requirements,

- Resources,

- The state of your quality systems,

- Competitive pressures,

- Internal and external costs,

- The size of your company,

- Number of sites,

- Management support,

- Internal cooperation, and

- The amount of documents to be generated.

SECURE INTERNAL SUPPORT

ISO 9000 registration is a team effort. Teams have been successfully used for project planning, product development, construction projects, quality improvement, sales enhancement, and other special activities. In the next section, we discuss how to organize for registration using a team-based approach.

STEP 5

ORGANIZE FOR REGISTRATION

Key Steps
• Determine the size of your team.
• Form an ISO 9000 self-managed team to coordinate registration.
• Identify critical planning, organizing, guiding, and controlling tasks.
• Select the team leader carefully.
• Communicate with management, employees, and other critical stakeholders about the direction and progress of the registration effort.
• Secure a commitment and resources from line operations.
• Resolve team and organizational conflicts quickly.
• Maintain enthusiasm and keep up the ISO 9000 momentum.
• Shift responsibility for maintaining ISO 9000 systems to the functional area involved or to maintenance teams on registration.

Research and experience have shown that interacting groups and teams consistently outperform individuals. Why? Teams allow for many different points of view to be articulated and shared. Team members develop more commitment to a project than traditional top-down, management-dictated projects. Teams often involve consensus decision making: everyone's views are heard; everyone is involved in planning, implementation, and results monitoring. Teams bring diverse skills, knowledge, and experiences to solving problems. Teams can be used positively to encourage skill building, ensure safety, improve the quality of work life, or improve organizational performance. Properly led, teams are a powerful force for improving operations. Improperly led, teams can be a toxin if they are used to coerce individuals to perform or conform.

WHAT IS AN ISO 9000 TEAM?

Teams go by several names, including cross-functional, multidisciplinary, high performance, quality improvement, project management, or self-managed. They consist of people with the skills, information, competencies, or education necessary to perform a specific task. The results are synergistic. The team develops skill sets that are more than the sum of single contributions.

In general, the ISO 9000 team is a high-performance, self-managed group of people with diverse skills who work toward a common goal—to attain ISO 9000 registration. It is a high-performance team because ISO 9000 has to be achieved within a short period of time. It is self-managed because the team is responsible and has the authority to facilitate registration or implementation.

Self-managed teams have several characteristics in common:

- They are small, with eight to ten members, depending on the size of the registration effort.

- Team membership is voluntary.

- Members have complementary skills.

- Members share a common purpose.

The goal of the ISO 9000 team is to manage the ISO 9000 registration effort within budget and on time. These are the main elements of success. However, success has other considerations:

- Resources are efficiently and effectively used.

- Teams are properly led and utilized.

- Corporate operations are minimally disrupted.

- Operational changes or proceduralization are smooth.

- ISO 9000 stakeholders are kept informed.

The size of a manageable team can vary from three to thirty or more people. A critical mass can be as few as seven committed members. The team consists of a team leader or facilitator and various members. Members are usually chosen from groups or departments that must comply with specific requirements of ISO 9001/9002/9003. For example, the purchasing department, a major ISO 9001 quality system requirement, may specify that the supplier must assess sub-contractors, develop specific purchasing information, and verify purchased products. A purchasing representative therefore should be on the team to interface and communicate requirements to the purchasing organization. The purchasing representative also may chair a subteam within the purchasing organization to ensure that all ISO 9000 requirements are satisfied.

THREE TYPES OF TEAMS: PROJECT, MAINTENANCE, AND FUNCTIONAL

ISO 9000 registration has two specific elements—achieving and maintaining registration. Three different types of teams may be involved with the registration and maintenance effort:

- The ISO 9000 registration team,

- The maintenance team, and

- The functional area teams.

THE ISO 9000 REGISTRATION TEAM

The ISO 9000 team is often a temporary project team. It has one objective—to achieve ISO 9000 registration by causing minimum organizational disruptions. Once registration is achieved, the registration team is disbanded. The project team establishes the systems and structure for ISO 9000 and organizes and manages the registration process. The team may develop, design, and document the required quality systems. Quality baselines are identified. ISO 9000 requirements are clarified. Resources are obtained. Gap analysis—analyzing the "what is" against the "what shall be"—is conducted. People are trained. Quality systems are implemented and documented.

Since this is a how-to-become-registered book, the discussion in this chapter centers on the project team, whose responsibility is to achieve ISO 9000 registration.

Critical Tasks of the ISO 9000 Registration Team

The ISO 9000 registration team has several critical functions:

PLANNING

- Become familiar with ISO 9000 and other requirements.
- Become familiar with customer and stakeholder requirements.
- Develop operating procedures for the team.
- Prepare the ISO 9000 registration budget.
- Prepare the ISO 9000 project schedule.
- Prepare the registration plan.
- Contact registrars.
- Review plans at critical milestones.
- Establish documentation and procedural baselines.
- Conduct gap analysis.

ORGANIZING

- Develop the team organization chart.
- Outline responsibilities, authorities, and restrictions.
- Select team members.
- Select an internal or external consultant.
- Review organizational requirements throughout project.
- Acquire line support.
- Acquire top management support.

(continued on next page)

Critical Tasks of the ISO 9000 Registration Team *(continued)*

GUIDING

- Guide work and the team to meet deadlines.

- Promote the project throughout the organization.

- Coach team members.

- Develop group decision-making processes.

- Establish objectives and goals.

- Promote team spirit.

- Resolve conflicts.

- Anticipate problems and conflicts.

CONTROLLING

- Develop project milestones.

- Monitor ISO 9000 project progress.

- Communicate progress to stakeholders.

- Maintain contact with the registrar.

- Report costs, schedule, and quality to stakeholders.

THE MAINTENANCE TEAM

The second type of team is a permanent one that ensures that quality systems are in place and operate properly. Maintenance of the registration requires quality systems to be monitored, and every six months or each year the organization is prepared for the surveillance audits.

What does the maintenance team do? Registration is not the final goal; the goal is continuous improvement. Quality systems must consistently be monitored. If discrepancies are found, they need to be corrected. This team works with the registrar to ensure that the surveillance audits are carried out effectively. This team also conducts ISO 9000 internal audits, supplies training, ensures that corrective actions are effective, and facilitates continuous quality improvement.

THE FUNCTIONAL AREA TEAMS

ISO 9000 requires significant people involvement, especially in functional areas that must monitor, maintain, and improve quality systems. In a small organization, one ISO 9000 team may be sufficient to guide the ISO 9000 registration effort. In a large organization of more than 200 employees, however, multiple teams may be needed to facilitate the effort. For example, each major department or functional area affected by an ISO 9000 clause may have a team to develop and write ISO 9000 process specific procedures.

The ISO 9000 registration team is responsible for managing and facilitating the entire project. In large registration efforts, the team is assisted by line personnel. Line personnel, often functional teams, are responsible for writing procedures and work instructions that comply with the intent and language of specific ISO 9000 quality system requirements.

In small organizations, the registration team may write many of the required procedures and work instructions. In large organizations, functional, business, and line groups may write the documentation with assistance from internal consultants, external consultants, or ISO 9000 team members. Functional groups should become involved because they are responsible for their own work processes and they know how work is really being conducted.

DO YOU NEED TO SET UP A FORMAL TEAM?

Do you need to set up a formal ISO 9000 team? Most small companies of less than thirty employees are seeking registration. In these operations, one individual may assume all the responsibilities for registration.

Certain questions immediately arise. Does this person have multiple responsibilities, such as for implementing a management information system, for training, for ISO 9000 registration, and for safety? Does this person have access to and the confidence of the small business owner? The advantage of the team approach is that responsibility and authority for an important task are shared among a group with multiple skills and resources dedicated achieving ISO 9000 registration.

GM Saturn Functional Teams

The GM Saturn plant has been an innovator in the development and implementation of operational work teams. At Saturn, a work unit is an integrated group of six to fifteen team members. Responsibility for work rests with the work unit, which may have as many as thirty work functions, including responsibilities usually assumed by management. These functions include designing jobs, conducting equipment maintenance, maintaining records, improving the area work process, determining work methods, assigning absentee replacements, performing repairs, conducting training, obtaining suppliers, and correcting system deficiencies. These functions require technical knowledge of the work, concern for the customer, commitment to quality, and mutual respect for other team members. The team applies its own knowledge to the problems, applies consensus decision making, and is responsible for all its work.[1]

ISO 9000 REGISTRATION TEAM STRUCTURE

The ISO 9000 registration team is responsible for managing the ISO 9000 registration process. It is made up of functional area representatives from organizational areas affected by specific ISO 9000 clauses who may chair subteams in their respective departments. Specific ISO 9000 quality systems detail design control, process control, inspection, and contract review requirements. Area and process-specific procedures and work instructions have to be developed in engineering, manufacturing, testing, and purchasing.

The ISO 9000 registration team is the driver of the registration effort. Success or failure is based on the team's effectiveness. A number of issues is critical in shaping the registration team:

- Authority and responsibilities,

- Reporting level,

- Team composition,

- Size of the team,

- Multiple responsibilities,

- Team member skills,

- Full- or part-time team members,

- Recruitment of team members, and

- Team training.

AUTHORITY AND RESPONSIBILITIES

The ISO 9000 team is responsible for managing the registration. ISO 9000 implementation is accomplished, for the most part, by people outside the registration team. The authority for accomplishing many of the tasks such as developing, implementing, and documenting the quality systems rests with others, specifically the operational groups that must comply with specific ISO 9001/9002/9003 requirements. These groups also are responsible for maintaining the quality systems after registration.

REPORTING LEVEL

Whom should the project team report to? The appropriate level is probably the one at which the request or authorization for ISO 9000 implementation is generated—such as the executive level, a steering committee, or a quality council. The ISO 9000 team may report to this level to

- Secure resources,

- Secure an official blessing,

- Secure internal cooperation,

- Communicate sufficient organizational status, visibility, and credibility, and

- Emphasize the importance of the organizational initiative.

TEAM COMPOSITION

Team composition is sometimes an area of contention. The objective of the team is to achieve ISO 9000 registration. The best way to achieve this should determine the composition of the team. Line managers may have to work with technical personnel and with line personnel.

In a hierarchical organization, having management representatives and workers on the same team may be problematic. Line managers and union personnel may not want to be on a work team together. Work agreements may even prohibit this. Engineering or product-testing managers may not want recommendations from users or others on how to conduct their work.

SIZE OF THE TEAM

The size of the team depends on the size of the organization seeking registration and the number of sites being registered. It is critical that the team be manageable and workable. Although the ISO 9000 registration team is responsible for leading and coordinating the preparation of the site for registration, responsibility and authority for the quality systems and their documentation still rest with the functional area.

As a general rule, every critical functional area addressed by a specific ISO 9001/9002/9003 clause should have a representative on the ISO 9000 registration team. This functional area representative to the team also may chair another implementation team in a functional area.

The person assigned to work with a functional area should be selected by the functional area team or supervisor. This person is trusted and has the knowledge to come back to his or her area to develop ISO 9000-complying procedures.

In a small organization, one ISO 9000 team may be sufficient to guide the ISO 9000 registration effort, but in larger organizations with multisite registrations, multiple teams may be established to facilitate the effort. Each major department or functional area, for example, may have a team to develop and write procedures.

MULTIPLE RESPONSIBILITIES

An ISO 9000 team member in a multisite registration effort may be a team member and also a functional employee, reporting vertically to the functional manager and horizontally to a team leader. ISO 9000 time commitments should be communicated and understood by the functional manager and the team leader. As part of the ISO 9000 team responsibilities, the team member participates in the ISO 9000 team's efforts and takes information back to a functional area, plant, or business unit. The team member then may establish a team within the functional area to disseminate information, develop procedures, or even lead the area's registration's efforts. This is similar to the train-the-trainer approach used in many organizations to vertically deliver information.

TEAM MEMBER SKILLS

Each person should bring unique skills and knowledge to the team. The person may have an ability, knowledge, experience, or skills that can be used in ISO 9000 registration or implementation.

ISO 9000 team membership requires basic technical and interpersonal competencies. The technical skills include ISO 9000, internal auditing, quality management, and operations skills, knowledge, and experience. Interpersonal skills include team building, project management, conflict resolution, and planning skills.

FULL- OR PART-TIME TEAM MEMBERS

Again, depending on the organization's size and other factors, the team membership can consist of the following:

- Full-time members,
- Part-time members, and
- Flexible members.

The preferred option often is to have one or more full-time members with other members who are part-timers who still perform their line functions. In a small company or small operation, one part-time person can conduct and manage

---

One Person Reporting to Multiple Bosses

A major organizational challenge occurs when one team member reports to two people—the ISO 9000 team leader and the line manager. This may result in divided loyalties, time commitments, and duties, which can be a recipe for trouble when there is an ISO 9000 and line activity conflict.

Consider the following scenario. You are the quality engineer for XYZ processing. Line personnel have been trained to solve problems, but process design problems are your responsibility. Tomorrow the registrar is conducting a preliminary assessment that has been scheduled for months. You are prepared, but there are problems on the line. Deficient products have been sent to the customer, who has to recall its products and demands immediate corrective action. The process operating team doesn't know how to fix the problem, so your boss, the manufacturing manager, demands that you rush over and fix the problem. Who wins—the customer with the problem or the team doing the preliminary assessment?

This situation may not be unusual. Although both the functional manager and the ISO 9000 team leader agree on the importance of ISO 9000 registration, there may be timing and other types of conflicts that must be resolved when they occur.

In this situation, the line problem is more critical than the ISO 9000 preassessment. No one on the ISO 9000 team is indispensable. The objective of the team is to share the responsibility and be able to cover for other members in preparing for and assisting in the audit.

---

the ISO 9000 activities. In a large multiplant registration effort, the ISO 9000 team will be composed largely of part-time members with a full-time staff.

One model frequently used in small organizations is to have a full-time team leader who does not manage the team according to the traditional definition of management but serves mainly as its administrative officer.

RECRUITMENT OF TEAM MEMBERS

ISO 9000 team members may volunteer or be assigned. Voluntary involvement ensures interest and commitment, but so can assignment. The culture and style of the organization may determine how employees are approached. In traditional organizations, the team leader and team members may be assigned to the ISO 9000 project. In participatory organizations, the team leader may be assigned, and members may be recruited and induced. Because ISO 9000 registration may require extra time, ISO 9000 team membership should be voluntary whenever possible.

Consider the following when recruiting team members:

- Explain the purpose and goal of ISO 9000 team participation and the commitment required of team members.

- Present benefits for the individual.

- Emphasize that individuals can decline team involvement.

- Answer all questions.

- Give individuals time to think about the proposal.

- Offer training and other resources for encouraging people to be part of the team.

- Guarantee that the person has a job to return to once the team's work is completed.

TEAM TRAINING

The ISO 9000 team requires specific ISO 9000 training, and all employees of the organization should be briefed on the ISO 9000 initiative. Let's first deal with ISO 9000 team training, which is specific and intense because team members integrate ISO 9000 quality systems throughout the organization. In large organizations, each team member may become the ISO 9000 team leader at his or her specific site, department, or work area. A typical training syllabus is presented in the next section (Step 6).

Technical knowledge and skills required by the ISO 9000 team include

- ISO 9000 fundamentals,

- Quality techniques and concepts,

- Process flowcharting,

- Internal auditing,

- Problem solving,

Successful Team Tips

Here are several guidelines for creating a successful ISO 9000 registration team:

- Keep the team small and manageable.
- Ensure that team member skills are complementary.
- Identify the goals and objectives of the project.
- Define and develop commitment for a common purpose.
- Maintain focus throughout implementation.
- Provide an enthusiastic team leader or facilitator.
- Encourage continuous involvement and feedback.
- Acknowledge or reward successes.
- Maintain the involvement of senior management.
- Identify organizational wins, such as how a change will improve the quality of work life.
- Provide feedback on performance, progress, and improvement opportunities.
- Make team contribution and participation part of the individual's appraisal.
- Balance work loads and prioritize.

- Pareto charting,
- Data collection,
- Project management,
- Fishbone diagrams,
- Procedure and work instruction preparation, and
- Process control.

Human relations skills required by the ISO 9000 team members include basic training in

- Human relations problem solving,

- Conflict resolution,

- Facilitating meetings,

- Project management, and

- Communication.

THE TEAM LEADER

Although the ISO 9000 team is nominally self-managed, a team leader or facilitator adds internal cohesion and direction and helps the team avoid being aimless and wasting resources. The ISO 9000 team leader is more coach, facilitator, and organizer than manager and performs the following functions:

- Defines the team's vision, mission, and objective,

- Develops plans for achieving these,

- Defines responsibilities and authorities,

- Obtains resources,

- Identifies milestones,

- Measures performance,

- Staffs the initiative,

- Establishes controls,

- Defines project milestones,

- Motivates personnel,

- Reports progress,

- Develops contingency plans, and

- Maintains flexibility.

What makes a good ISO 9000 team leader? Some organizations choose a technical project manager with strong management and technical skills. Some choose an operating manager with a staff, technical, or operating background. Sometimes a human resource person with coaching, facilitating, and communications skills is selected because ISO 9000 implementation may involve organizational change.

The team leader may assume various roles, including

- Champion,
- Administrator and manager,
- Planner,
- Facilitator,
- Salesperson,
- Negotiator,
- Mediator, and
- Coordinator.

CHAMPION

Sometimes a senior manager is assigned to be the ISO 9000 champion and team leader, but championing and leading the ISO 9000 team may appear to be a conflict of interest. The ISO 9000 team leader may appear to be promoting himself or herself instead of the virtues of ISO 9000 registration. For this reason, the two functions often are separated.

ADMINISTRATOR AND MANAGER

The team leader may serve as both administrator and manager by planning, organizing, guiding, and controlling the team. This involves filling out paper work, arranging for resources, presenting reports, or managing meetings.

Managing meetings is a major challenge for the team leader. Meetings are important for conveying information or for developing consensus. Because so many meetings lose focus and wander, many organizations are training line employees, process engineers, supervisors, or rank and file workers in how to facilitate ISO 9000 meetings.

PLANNER

The team leader is also a planner. With the team, the leader may lead the development of a tactical plan for achieving registration. The plan is a road map defining the intermediate steps in the journey. However, one person, usually the team leader, has to set the registration project in motion. Effective planning goes beyond developing a plan with schedules and budgets. The team must communicate its resource requirements, management commitment, support needs, and other requirements.

FACILITATOR

The team leader is probably more facilitator than manager. The team facilitator encourages team commitment, individual involvement, and forward movement in the registration process. If an individual is hindering progress, then the team leader or facilitator may intervene to correct problems. The objective is to keep moving forward to secure ISO 9000 registration.

Some teams work well when a trained facilitator from outside the team is available to resolve differences. The facilitator may be a staff person from the human resources, quality, or training departments and should understand group dynamics and have the respect of the organization. This person also should have good observation and intervention skills and a good understanding of how teams develop, work, and get things done and be able to capture these qualities to maintain forward movement.

SALESPERSON

Since the ISO 9000 team leader has no direct line authority, line or functional management may not want to work with the ISO 9000 team. In a small organization, this is not likely. However, in a large organization with multiple business units, divisions, and plants, specific site ISO 9000 implementation and registration may be optional or at the discretion of the line manager. In these cases, the ISO 9000 team leader or the team members have to sell the benefits and advantages of ISO 9000 registration to line management and employees. With more responsibility being downloaded onto these independent business units, if the plant manager or the business unit manager doesn't understand or see the advantages of registration, he or she may not want to assist implementation or become registered.

In a large organization with five or many more entirely different product lines, each business unit manager will look at and analyze the benefits of registration based on customer requirements, market conditions, and other factors. This decision may be entirely independent of what other business units are doing in terms of registration. The ISO 9000 team manager has to sell the benefits of ISO 9000 registration to this manager.

NEGOTIATOR

Negotiating skills are some of the important skills needed by both the team leader and team members. The team leader must communicate the importance of ISO 9000 registration and obtain resources from line management. In large organizations, team members will themselves become team leaders in their respective functional areas. These people must have the ability to communicate effectively and to work with people to develop quality documentation.

As mentioned above, the team is in a classic management quandary. The team has responsibility for ISO 9000 registration but may not have the authority to implement quality systems in the organization. At most, the team may have senior management's blessing on the project. The team and its members must negotiate with the line and functional management of the organization to implement and document quality systems.

MEDIATOR

Conflict may arise in the ISO 9000 registration process. Deadlines are missed. Operations are disrupted. Conflict may arise between the ISO 9000 manager and line managers about interpreting ISO 9000 clauses or allocating monies. If they are not amicably and effectively resolved, conflicts can result in poor decision making, personality conflicts, delays, dead ends, and other disruptions.

Management Tips for the Team Leader

The following time management tips will make your registration easier:

- *Plan the registration.* Discuss and try to develop consensus on the issues addressed in the planning stage.

- *Follow the plan.* The plan does not have to be perfect and will evolve during the process.

- *Develop a Project Evaluation and Review Technique (PERT) or Critical Path Method (CPM) chart.* These project planning charts detail the steps, timelines, and sometimes the responsibilities of who is going to do what during the registration process.

- *Assign responsibilities.* Each team member probably represents an area that must comply with ISO 9001/9002/9003 requirements. Functional area representatives must know what they are supposed to do and who does what.

- *Conduct a time analysis.* Estimate realistically how long each ISO 9000 activity should take, and place these estimates on a PERT chart.

- *Classify and prioritize activities.* Focus the team on the tasks that are important to achieve ISO 9000 registration.

- *Empower team members.* Empower team members to make decisions and provide training.

- *Communicate electronically.* Excessive paperwork can hinder the project. Keep lines of communication open through electronic or other means.

- *Use management by exception.* Allow the team members to do what must be done. Intervene only if there are problems.

The mediator is an important role for the ISO 9000 registration leader. The manager must understand group interaction dynamics, discern causes of friction, and be able to propose solutions that maintain motivation. Occasionally, conflict is beneficial, however, such as competitiveness over solving problems or offering the most suggestions for improvement.

COORDINATOR

In a multisite registration, teams may be formed at each site. A corporate team should be formed to coordinate on-site preparation, planning, and assessments. Again, the corporate team members become the facilitators, leaders, or coordinators of the ISO 9000 effort in their respective sites. The key to ensuring registration success is good communications which is discussed in the next section.

THE KEY TO ORGANIZING: GOOD COMMUNICATION

Deming declared that unity of purpose is important for the development of a quality management system, such as ISO 9000. How is unity of purpose established and maintained? The only way to keep the registration initiative on track and moving forward is through open communication.

Good communication serves the following purposes. It

- Informs employees about the value of registration in terms important to them, such as making work easier or safer,

- Creates a positive climate for ISO 9000 implementation,

- Develops vision and mission statements for ISO 9000 registration,

- Defines goals and objectives, and

- Defines ISO 9000 responsibilities and authorities for business units, departments, teams, and individuals.

Poor communication is the biggest problem in registration. Registration may result in additional work in developing procedures or may result in process changes. Change is difficult for organizations and may result in fear, apathy, or obstacles.

The following illustrates a potential communications problem. The ISO 9000 registration initiative may require a team composed of workers and management to collaborate in the ISO 9000 registration. These teams may work well as long as a manager or his or her employees are not overly critical or sensitive of each other. An overly sensitive manager may learn things that he or she didn't want to know. An overly critical manager may stifle candor. Employees may feel reluctant to open up if they think their jobs are jeopardized.

A positive, open team should focus on securing commitment and involvement from all employees. This benefits both supervisors and employees. Workers learn that management is concerned about their welfare and not simply interested in production quotas and cost reduction.

The level of communication is a strong predictor of ISO 9000 registration success. Employees, supervisors, managers and the entire organization gain from the planned and informal interaction of all personnel for the success of the project. ISO 9000 quality systems involve different departments, each of which has its own priorities, agenda, and personalities. Successful, cost-effective registration is the result of collaboration, cooperation, and communication.

Early on, the team leader should convey basic information to every volunteer or assigned member of the team by

- Explaining ISO 9000,

- Explaining the objectives of the registration effort,

- Emphasizing the organizational value and benefits of registration,

- Stressing the personal value and benefits of being part of the team,

- Identifying other team members,

- Explaining why the team member was assigned or asked to volunteer,

- Explaining the duties and obligations to team members,

- Explaining the required commitment, and

- Ensuring that the team member has a job to return to.

A frank and objective discussion while the team is forming can preempt misunderstandings later in the ISO 9000 project. The more a team member knows, the more he or she will be committed to the project. An important objective to this early discussion is to set the stage for team cooperation and collaboration. The team leader is setting an example where trust can be developed. As the project progresses, team members should feel comfortable about sharing information.

HOW TO WORK WITH FUNCTIONAL GROUPS

The registration mandate can't be thrown over the fence to an isolated ISO 9000 project team. Because the ISO 9000 team does not have the corporate resources to write documentation and implement the quality systems, it has to work with functional groups.

HOW TO OBTAIN RESOURCES

The ISO 9000 team relies on the resources of the organization and other departments to get much of the ISO 9000 work done. How does the team obtain assistance? First, the organization must emphasize the importance of ISO 9000 registration and how it will affect the business as a whole. The ISO 9000 team probably doesn't have the resources or personnel to write the required policies, procedures, and work instructions. Unless people are assigned to these activities,

---

Critical Considerations for the ISO 9000 Team

The following are issues for the ISO 9000 team to consider:

- The team's formal position within the organization,
- Authorities and responsibilities,
- Allocation and control of funds,
- Selection of team members,
- Selection of a registrar,
- Authority to resolve conflicts,
- Authority to develop a plan,
- Maintaining liaisons with stakeholders,
- Cutting red tape, and
- Defining interfaces within organizations.

registration will take much longer. Only line management has the resources to assign to these tasks. Procedures and work instructions are all process and operations specific. Line management has to be willing to assign employees who can work as part of the ISO 9000 team and bring knowledge and skills that will assist registration. Either directly or through example, top management has to convince operational and functional units to assist the registration effort.

Organization Traps

The team is responsible for facilitating the ISO 9000 registration project within budget and on schedule. Time management is one of the project's critical components. Often, cost and time overruns go hand in hand. The registration may take longer because of

- Numerous meetings,

- Lack of organizational commitment,

- Lack of management commitment,

- Lack of resources,

- Registrar unavailability,

- Conflict resolution,

- Continuous planning, replanning, and more planning,

- Ineffective implementation and execution,

- Lack of quality systems,

- Excessive procedure and work instruction writing,

- Protection of resources and information,

- Personality or other conflict among team members,

- Lack of resources,

(continued on next page)

Organization Traps (*continued*)

- Communication problems,

- Work overloads,

- Scheduling conflicts,

- Personality conflicts,

- Accountability or authority conflicts,

- Unrealistic scheduling or delivery dates,

- Critical areas or project bottlenecks,

- Inexperience,

- Lack of operations support,

- False starts, and

- Differences between accountability and authority.

INDIVIDUAL AND TEAM EMPOWERMENT

ISO 9000 registration succeeds in an organizational environment that encourages and rewards teamwork. ISO 9000 planning, documentation, and proceduralization should be understood as providing important organizational benefits. Middle management, supervision, technical, and line personnel are the most knowledgeable about their operations and should have the most investment in registration success.

Team and individual empowerment allows people to make decisions and implement changes that improve the quality of work life, improve safety, or enhance operating efficiencies. Empowerment becomes important in promoting, implementing, documenting, and maintaining quality systems. Empowerment cannot be imposed from the top or outside the work area. It must start in the work area at the individual and team levels.

Line management and the team should have a mutually supportive relationship. This may be difficult because of conflicting objectives: line supervision wants to maintain operations, and the ISO 9000 team wants to establish quality systems that may change or disrupt operations. The ISO 9000 team should explain that quality systems are a more effective means to control operations. Line management may perceive that the ISO 9000 team is dictating systems that line personnel doesn't want.

The ISO 9000 registration team can convey powerful messages about how ISO 9000 implementation can improve everyone's work life by:

- Writing ISO 9000 procedures and work instructions that allow employees or team members to define how they will perform their work,

- Defining how work will be managed, supervised, controlled, planned, and measured, which previously were management functions,

- Defining the role of staff and support activities, and

- Redesigning reward and recognition systems.

The ISO 9000 registration effort may flag because of time, resource, and other requirements. In the next section, we discuss how to maintain momentum.

MAINTAINING MOMENTUM

As organizations restructure through reengineering or proceduralization, they go through wrenching changes:

- Fewer people are available to do the work.

- People have more authority and responsibility.

- Organizations are flatter and more democratic.

- Middle management and staff disappear.

- Bureaucracies and departments wither away.

- Employee allegiance and loyalty disappear.

- Communications are more horizontal.

In organizations that survive downsizing, commitment and enthusiasm are difficult to obtain from team members, who often have had the difficult and painful experience of seeing their fellow employees outplaced. The challenge for top management is to obtain the commitment of individuals and teams for ISO 9000 registration. Criticism and inertia must be dispelled. Criticisms such as "This too shall pass," "I've seen this before," and "I've got too much on my plate already" make registration more difficult and more costly.

Maintaining ISO 9000 motivation is a major challenge for the team. Interest can wane because of the amount of work, multiple projects, internal resistance, poor leadership, misdirection, no follow up, low-level quality systems, or nonexistent quality systems.

A top-level manager may serve as the original sponsor and champion. This person may facilitate

- "What is" and the "benefits of" discussion workshops,

- "How to" implement discussion workshops, and

- Training-the-trainer workshops.

How are team members kept motivated when their time may be fragmented among several projects? For more employees, work is no longer a forty-hour week; it involves more responsibility and authority and continues until a job is done. This may take up to sixty hours a week, which for supervisors is often uncompensated. These people are difficult to motivate over the long haul and must be motivated through increased challenges, bonuses, freedom, or authority.

Team building and maintenance requires tender loving care. It does not develop without effort. Cute slogans, posters, or catch phrases won't work. There must be strong group rapport and a general spirit of excitement to support the registration effort. Otherwise, the registration process may become a grind. Hours are long, especially if registration duties are imposed on employees. To help nurture a positive spirit, top management and the team leader can

- Recognize participation,

- Praise often and genuinely,

- Assign specific short-term tasks,

- Measure attainment,

- Hold frequent progress meetings,

- Maintain information flows,

- Obtain internal or external assistance, and

- Communicate successes, tips, and other helps.

In the next Step we discuss ISO 9000 training and education.

Early Warning Signs

Some early warning signs can alert you to the fact that ISO 9000 registration may not be going smoothly, specifically

- Missed deadlines,

- Changes in team performance,

- Communication problems,

- Unclear objectives,

- Operational objection and resistance,

- Increased corrective action,

- Unstable processes,

- Numerous preassessment deficiencies,

- Slow corrective action,

- Finger pointing,

- Lack of enthusiasm or commitment,

- Increased game playing or turf battles,

- Sabotage or foot dragging, and

- Lack of direction.

Is there one correct method to deal with all or each one of these early warning signs? No. However, each one may be anticipated and discussed. A consensus can be reached about the existence of the problems, an action plan can be developed to address and solve the problem, and the effectiveness of the resolution of the problem can be monitored.

STEP 6

TRAIN AND EDUCATE

Key Steps
• Introduce ISO 9000 concepts and purposes to everyone in the organization.
• Link ISO 9000 registration to important external forces, such as customer or regulatory requirements.
• Integrate ISO 9000 registration with other organizational initiatives.
• Stress the importance of the learning organization.
• Ensure training is organization, process and system, and product specific.
• Obtain consulting assistance, if necessary.

ISO 9000 registration often is linked with ongoing efforts outside the scope of ISO 9000 registration, such as total quality management or other continuous improvement initiatives.

INTEGRATING REGISTRATION WITH OTHER INITIATIVES

ISO 9000 registration often is coupled with other organization-enhancing initiatives. New systems and processes that require training are constantly being integrated or imposed on the organization.

When ISO 9000 registration or implementation does not have sufficient urgency, it may be piggybacked with another organization initiative. ISO 9000 registration is sometimes linked with

- Total quality management,
- Customer and supplier certification,
- Reengineering processes,
- Flexible and adaptable organizations,
- High-performance and self-managed teams,
- Concurrent product development, and
- Lifelong learning.

TOTAL QUALITY MANAGEMENT

ISO 9000 registration involves many total quality management technologies. For example, ISO 9000 can serve as the foundation or platform for quality control leading to a total quality management system. ISO 9000 proceduralization through quality systems implementation ensures that deficiencies don't occur. If they do, then deficiencies are corrected quickly and resolutely.

CUSTOMER AND SUPPLIER CERTIFICATION

ISO 9001/9002/9003 are customer and supplier requirements. Many well known customer-supplier certification initiatives such as those in the auto industry are using ISO 9001 as the foundation for their customer-supplier partnerships.

REENGINEERING PROCESSES

Efficiency and effectiveness are the management objectives of all organizations in the 1990s. ISO 9000 proceduralization and reengineering go hand in hand. Reengineering focuses on dividing functional business units into process units. This may require redeploying workers in multidisciplinary teams that concentrate on getting the right products and services to the customer just in time. Once ISO 9000 quality systems are developed and documented, teams can develop and document quality systems.

FLEXIBLE AND ADAPTABLE ORGANIZATION

Competitiveness pressures are forcing all organizations to be flexible and adaptable:

- Customer satisfaction throughout the product life cycle is paramount.

- Products and services must be developed quickly.

- Multifunctional organizations, sometimes called *virtual partnerships*, are a favored means for developing products or delivering services quickly.

- Quality systems are developed and documented to ensure that processes are capable of meeting requirements.

- If there is a deficiency, it is corrected immediately.

- Periodic process and system auditing ensures that deficiencies don't recur.

HIGH-PERFORMANCE AND SELF-MANAGED TEAMS

Senior management is asking why first-line and middle managers are needed when an employee team can perform many of their functions. Senior management is also asking why a senior manager should lead the ISO 9000 registration initiative when it can be secured by a self-managed team.

CONCURRENT PRODUCT DEVELOPMENT

In the traditional sequential method of developing products, marketing identified customer needs, engineering designed products, purchasing found suppliers, manufacturing produced the product, and distribution delivered the product to customers. Each functional area was an organizational silo that sequentially contributed to product development. The process was bureaucratic and slow.

Time is now a competitive weapon. Products and services are delivered just in time to please customers. Sequential product development is giving way to simultaneous or concurrent development. Multidisciplinary product development teams work to develop products. ISO 9000 quality systems establish a structure to ensure that quality is specified and controlled throughout the development process.

LIFELONG LEARNING

A learning organization encourages collaborative and collective learning from all employees. Lifelong learning and skill building are essential in the rapidly changing competitive environment. Markets are fast-moving streams. To survive and prosper, companies and individuals must satisfy customers with aesthetic, defect-free products.

The Importance of a Learning Organization

Fundamental to the learning organization is the belief that increasing the skill level of the entire organization is critical to business success. International competition is requiring companies to achieve ISO 9000 registration. Competition requires higher quality, lower cost, more variety, customization, higher convenience, and higher aesthetics. As the competitive bar is raised, companies must satisfy and surpass these requirements.

Higher employee skills are necessary. Some studies reveal that up to 20 percent of the workforce is nonfunctional. Many companies have to teach such basic skills as reading, computing, writing, cooperation, problem solving, and quality control. More training is now occurring in the workplace than in many schools as organizations are making significant investments in training to implement new initiatives, such as ISO 9000.

THE ISO 9000 LEARNING ORGANIZATION

Often, ISO 9000 registration is linked with improving and encouraging organizational learning. The learning organization encourages collaborative learning, thinking, and doing. Individual improvement leads to team, process, and organizational competitiveness.

ISO 9000 TRAINING

Training is one of the twenty quality system requirements of ISO 9001. The quality system requirement states that a company must have procedures in place to identify and provide training for all employees whose activities affect quality. The ISO 9001 clause does not specify what training, except that it must satisfy the organizational needs for quality. If all employees are responsible for the quality of their work, then just about everyone should be trained. To illustrate the requirements and concerns in a service operation, customer service personnel must

- Understand customer needs and expectations,

- Be able to satisfy these requirements,

- Be prompt and courteous,

- Communicate properly,

- Handle customer complaints, and

- Overcome resistance and other negative attitudes.

While all companies pursuing registration are training employees to meet ISO 9001/9002/9003 quality requirements, more companies are cross-training and going much further than simply meeting ISO 9000 requirements. Most high-performance team members are encouraged to learn multiple jobs. Pay is often tied to learning. These efforts—sometimes called *pay for knowledge*—focus on ensuring that team members have multiple value-adding skills.

The objective is to have employees be able to perform multiple tasks if another employee is sick or leaves or if production requirements change. For example, when a company receives a contract for new products, personnel with varied skills can move rapidly to produce the new products. If a problem occurs, the employee is equipped to solve the problem even when the cause is outside the person's regular job.

The company gains as well as the individual. The individual is paid to learn new skills that may be transferable to other areas of the organization or even outside the organization. Today there's no such thing as job security. Jobs and people are mobile, and people migrate to jobs offering the most pay, freedom, and quality of work. Having multiple marketable skills facilitates job mobility.

ORGANIZATIONAL ISO 9000 TRAINING

The way to prepare teams and their employees for ISO 9000 registration is through training. Middle-management, supervision, and line employees are introduced to and trained in

- The purpose and benefits of ISO 9000 registration,

- ISO 9000 principles, terms, and purpose,

- Problem-solving skills,

- Procedure and work instruction development, and

- Basic statistical process control.

Training is site and process specific. People must know their jobs if they are to develop realistic, useable, and useful procedures and work instructions. All too often, policies, procedures, and work instructions have been on the shelf for, say, the last ten years, never revised or even followed.

ISO 9000 TEAM TRAINING

ISO 9000 team members require basic technical and interpersonal competencies. The technical skills include ISO 9000, internal auditing, and documentation writing knowledge. Interpersonal skills include team building, project management, conflict resolution, and planning skills. Internal auditing knowledge is required to satisfy two ISO 9000 quality system requirements—internal auditing and correction action. Internal auditing also is the means for conducting the gap analysis or preassessment that determines where a company is in relation to ISO

9000 requirements. For more specific knowledge, one or more people may attend a five-day lead assessor training course, which trains people to conduct the registration audits. Typical course outlines for these courses are shown on pages 97–98.

Outline of an Internal Auditing Course

1. Quality Auditing

   What is a quality audit?

   Seven types of quality assessments

   Twenty-one benefits of quality auditing

2. Organizing for a Quality Audit

   Key players in the quality audit

   Organizing the quality audit

   Determining when the audit should be conducted

3. Planning the Quality Audit

   Understanding the customer's quality requirements

   Identifying the auditee's quality requirements

   Developing a preliminary quality survey

   Tips for planning an audit

   Identifying and evaluating internal controls

   Preparing the quality audit plan

4. Conducting the Quality Audit

   Compliance with quality standards

   Six areas of internal control

   Testing for internal control

   Tips for conducting an audit

   Six techniques for gathering evidence

   Audit management, engineering, purchasing, and manufacturing

(continued on next page)

Outline of an Internal Auditing Course (*continued*)

---

5. Reporting the Quality Audit Results

   Major types of quality audit reports

   Essential elements of a standard audit report

   Tips for reporting the audit

   Reporting positive and negative findings

Outline of a Lead Assessor Course

---

1. Quality Auditing System Assessment

   Function of quality assurance

   Elements of a quality system

   Quality documentation, including quality manual, procedures, and work instructions

2. Understanding ISO 9000 Quality Requirements

   Describing and understanding ISO 9000 requirements

   Understanding the relationships among ISO 9001/9002/9003

3. Quality Auditing

   Responsibilities of the three parties of the audit

   The process of quality auditing

   Different types of quality assessments

4. Preaudit Activities

   Planning audit activities

   Developing a checklist

(*continued on next page*)

Outline of a Lead Assessor Course (*continued*)

   Performing a preassessment visit

   Conducting an opening meeting

5. Conducting the Audit

   Collecting objective evidence

   Evaluating information and evidence

   Techniques for listening and questioning

6. Postaudit and Follow Up

   How to conduct a closing meeting

   Writing an effective audit report

   Issuing noncompliance forms

   Issuing corrective action requests

   How to assess corrective action

   Close out noncompliance

   How to conduct surveillance audit

WHO CONDUCTS THE TRAINING?

Outside consultants, internal experts, or supervisors can supply ISO 9000 training. Front-line supervisors and managers are also excellent ISO 9000 instructors. Technical knowledge and interpersonal skills are the major prerequisites for a good trainer. Managers may use this opportunity to change their style from an authority-based style to one based on assisting, mentoring, and encouraging self-directed work teams.

To show commitment, senior managers may lead train-the-trainer seminars introducing the purpose and benefits of registration or implementation. A senior manager may work with an external consultant who serves as the organization's implementation facilitator. Once the initial training is conducted, trainers train their own staffs and so on down through the organizational hierarchy. Train-the-trainer seminars are an effective means of transferring ISO 9000 knowledge, information, and skills.

NEED FOR CONSULTING

ISO 9000 registration evangelists are shouting the virtues of registration. Many sincerely sing the praises of ISO 9000 registration, but often their background and experience is deficient. Many people enter the field with only a superficial knowledge of quality and the quality systems they are consulting in. The demand for experienced ISO 9000 consultants simply exceeds supply.

Industry- or process-specific ISO 9000 implementation also may require special expertise. This book presents a general approach to registration, but some registrations may require that a consultant have an industry-specific background. Medical devices, natural gas appliances, and other industry categories, for example, require regulatory knowledge beyond the scope of a general book. A good consultant should know your industry, processes, and products foremost and also have a strong ISO 9000 and quality background. You may not have to hire a consultant if your size, processes, quality level, or products don't require specialized knowledge or experience.

In the next Step we discuss how to conduct a preassessment.

STEP 7

CONDUCT THE PREASSESSMENT

Key Steps
• Understand ISO 9000 quality system requirements.
• Communicate the importance of quality system controls to functional units.
• Determine which ISO 9000 standard—ISO 9001/9002/9003—is right for you.
• Determine the current status of quality systems, often called determining the "what is."
• Determine what "shall be" as specified by ISO 9001/9002/9003.
• Close the gap between the "what is" and "what shall be" by developing quality documentation.
• Break down ISO 9000 requirements into organizational and functional elements.
• Have the ISO 9000 registration team develop organizational policies and procedures.
• Have functional units develop or contribute actively to writing departmental or work-specific procedures and instructions.
• Develop corrective actions for major and minor discrepancies.

The preassessment, also called an *internal audit*, determines an organization's ability to become registered. The preassessment basically compares "what is" being done against "what shall be" done as required by ISO 9001/9002/9003. The preassessment begins with an understanding of what ISO 9001/9002/9003 specify.

UNDERSTANDING ISO 9001/9002/9003

The International Organization for Standardization (ISO) was founded in 1946 and is headquartered in Switzerland. It consists of more than ninety member nations. The U.S. representative to the ISO 9000 is the American National Standards Institute, a private standards-making body in the United States. The ISO 9000 family of standards has been adopted by the majority of the ISO 9000 members and probably will be adopted by all members by the end of the decade.

The standards go by various names. In the United States, they are published as the Q90 or Q9000 series, and in Europe they are called the European Norm (EN) 29000 series. Their designation changes throughout the world, but they are technically similar. This book doesn't explain the ISO 9000 family of standards, but you can learn more about them from many of the "what is" ISO 9000 books, including my own *ISO 9000.*

ISO 9000 is a family or series of standards. They can be divided into two groups—the "shall" and the "should" standards. The "shall" standards are listed on page 104: ISO 9000 Standards. These are the two-party, contractual documents between a customer and a supplier. ISO 9000 serves as the table of contents for the other three standards—ISO 9001/9002/9003. ISO 9001 is the most comprehensive of the standards and covers twenty quality system requirements. ISO 9001 is used "when conformance to specified requirements is to be assured by the supplier during several stages," which may include design/development, production, installation, and servicing. ISO 9002 is primarily used by the supplier during production and installation. ISO 9003 is used when the supplier assures quality solely at final inspection and test.[1] (See Figure 7.1.)

IT'S THE SYSTEM

ISO 9001/9002/9003 consists of a family of quality system requirements. The standard defines a quality system as the "organizational structure, responsibilities, procedures, process and resources for implementing quality management."[2]

The systems element is integrated and illustrated in several ways in the family of standards:

FIGURE 7.1
ISO 9001/9002/9003 Structure

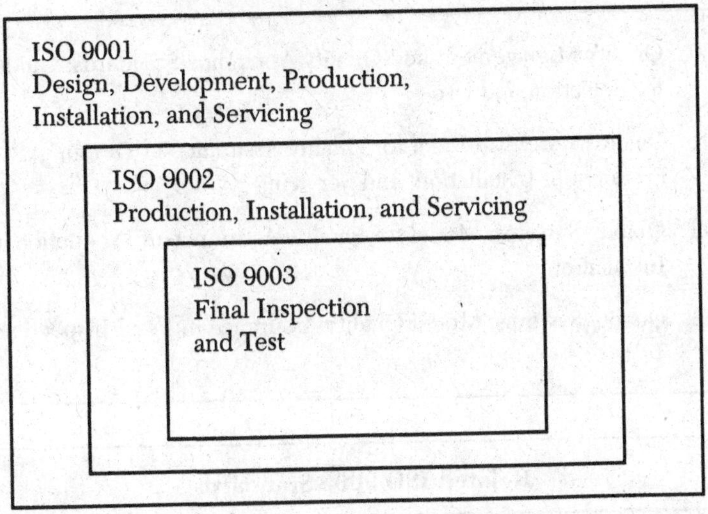

ISO 9001
Design, Development, Production,
Installation, and Servicing

ISO 9002
Production, Installation, and Servicing

ISO 9003
Final Inspection
and Test

- Quality systems form loops for detecting, reinforcing, and correcting. For example, using systems for internal auditing and corrective action, you can find and correct problems.

- Quality systems clauses can affect multiple quality system requirements. For example, documentation is required in nearly every quality system.

- Control of operations is inherent throughout the series.

- Quality system requirements of ISO 9001 follow a value-adding chain from design, manufacturing, purchasing, production, and servicing to storage and delivery.

- Quality terms and concepts are defined precisely in ISO 8402. This ensures common interpretation and usage throughout the world.

REVISIONS

ISO 9001/9002/9003 were developed in 1987. Although the standards are supposed to be revised every four or five years, the first revisions came out in 1994. Probably less than ten percent of ISO 9001 was changed or clarified. The major changes occurred in ISO 9003. Only four out of the twenty quality system

ISO 9000 Standards

ISO 9000 Quality Management and Quality Assurance Standards: Guidelines for Selection and Use

ISO 9001 Quality Systems: Model for Quality Assurance in Design, Production, Installation, and Servicing

ISO 9002 Quality Systems: Model for Quality Assurance in Production and Installation

ISO 9003 Quality Systems: Model Quality Assurance in Final Inspection and Test

Related ISO 9000 Standards

Note: Some of the ISO 9000 standards have been adopted; others are going through the review-consensus cycle.

ISO 9000-3 Guidelines for the Application of ISO 9001 to the Development, Supply, and Maintenance of Software

ISO 9004 Quality Management and Quality Systems Elements: Guidelines

ISO 9004-2 Quality Management and Quality System Elements, Part 2: Guidelines for Services

ISO 9004-3 Quality Management and Quality System Elements, Part 3: Guidelines for Processed Materials

ISO 9004-4 Quality Management and Quality System Elements, Part 4: Guidelines for Quality Improvement

ISO 9004-5 Quality Management and Quality System Elements, Part 5: Guidelines for Quality Plans

ISO 9004-6 Quality Management and Quality System Elements, Part 6: Guidelines for Quality Assurance for Project Management

ISO 9004-7 Quality Management and Quality System Elements, Part 7: Guidelines for Quality System Requirements for Configuration Management

Related ISO 9000 Standards (*continued*)	
ISO 9004-8	Quality Management and Quality System Elements, Part 8: Guidelines for Quality Principles
ISO 10011-1	Guidelines for Auditing Quality Systems, Part 1: Auditing
ISO 10011-2	Guidelines for Auditing Quality Systems, Part 2: Qualification Criteria for Auditors
ISO 10011-3	Guidelines for Auditing Quality Systems, Part 3: Managing Audit Programs
ISO 10012-1	Guidelines for Quality Assurance Requirements for Measuring Equipment, Part 1: Metrological Quality System for Measuring Equipment
ISO 10012-2	Guidelines for Quality Assurance Requirement for Measuring Equipment, Part 2: Quality Assurance
ISO 10013	Guidelines for Preparation of a Quality Manual
ISO 10014	Guidelines for Economics of Quality Management
ISO 10015	Guidelines for Continuing Education and Training
ISO 10016	Guidelines for Quality Documents

requirements were significantly revised. This book describes the registration process—how to implement, achieve, and maintain registration—and it's a process that can be used with any future revision of the standards. The details that a company has to comply with may be modified, but the process of complying stays the same.

HOW TO DETERMINE COMPLIANCE

Determining which standard to comply with can be confusing. In general, if you design products or parts, then pursue ISO 9001 registration, which is the most comprehensive of the contractual standards. If you work primarily in a production operation, such as assembly, then register to ISO 9002. If your company primarily uses final inspection and testing to assure quality, then ISO 9003 is your standard.

Registration is primarily by site. However, there are exceptions. Some sites may have multiple product lines under one roof or in one location. In these cases, multiple certificates are issued—one for each distinct production line.

In some cases, one certificate may cover multiple sites if each site follows the same quality manual and has similar procedures. In other words, each site has parallel quality systems and uses a similar quality manual. Typical examples include distribution centers, sales offices, and gas stations, where each site does the same thing in much the same way. Before you jump into pursuing multisite registration, however, seek the advice of a registrar or an ISO 9000 professional. The risk is that if one of the sites is found to have recurring discrepancies, then all sites risk the possible suspension of certification even though the other sites conform to the particular ISO 9000 requirements.

WHO DOES WHAT?

The ISO 9000 team should first identify the department having nominal responsibility and authority to address, satisfy, and maintain compliance with the particular functional or department clause being examined.

Who does what in terms of ISO 9001 implementation? The ISO 9000 registration team has to answer this critical question if the entire organization is to be involved in implementation and procedural writing. The first challenge is to divide the standard into general and functional quality system requirements and clauses. Once this is done, quality systems procedures and work instructions can be assigned to the specific functional areas. Quality documentation covering the entire organization is usually the responsibility of the ISO 9000 registration team.

The standard's quality system requirements can be divided into these two broad classifications—(1) organizational and management or (2) function- and department-specific. Some special clauses are even more specific.

The organizational and management quality system requirements are

4.1   Management responsibility

4.2   Quality system

4.3   Contract review

4.5   Document and data control

4.16   Control of quality records

4.17   Internal quality audits

4.18   Training

4.20   Statistical techniques

The functional- and department-specific quality system requirements are:

4.4   Design control

4.6   Purchasing

4.7   Control of customer-supplied product

4.8   Product identification and traceability

4.9   Process control

4.10   Inspection and testing

4.11   Control of inspection, measuring, and test equipment

4.12   Inspection and test status

4.13   Control of nonconforming product

4.14   Corrective and preventive action

4.15   Handling, storage, packaging, preservation, and delivery

4.19   Servicing

Each subclause under quality system requirements also covers similar issues. For example, the "management responsibility" quality system requirement also deals with company wide issues:

4.1   Management responsibility

4.1.1   Quality policy

4.1.2   Organization

4.1.2.1 Responsibility and authority

4.1.2.2 Resources

4.1.2.3   Management representative

4.1.3   Management review

In the same way, the "inspection and testing" quality system requirement deals with specific functional quality assurance issues:

4.10   Inspection and testing

4.10.1   General

4.10.2   Receiving inspection and testing

4.10.3   In-process inspection and testing

4.10.4   Final inspection and testing

4.10.5   Inspection and test records

WRITING QUALITY POLICIES, PROCEDURES AND WORK INSTRUCTIONS

The quality manual, the first-level quality documentation, consists of companywide quality policies and documentation that reflects ISO 9001/9002/9003 requirements. Organize the quality manual so there is one-to-one mapping from each quality system requirement and clause to the section to the quality manual. In other words, Section 1 of your quality manual corresponds to Section 4.1 of the quality system requirements—"management responsibility." The registrar's quality audit team will check your compliance to ISO 9001 by assessing your quality manual section by section against the appropriate ISO 9001/9002/9003 clause. (See Figure 7.2.)

The next two levels of quality documentation are specific to the site's quality systems, processes, and products. Procedures and work instructions are written as to how work is conducted, not as it should be. This is an important distinction. The auditor may sample this level of quality documentation by assessing whether what is written in procedures and work instructions is actually done.

If things are done differently than what is required by the standard, should operations change or somehow be modified? ISO 9001 is not an operations document. It prescribes broad quality system requirements for the purpose of controlling quality. The supplier must determine how the specifics of the ISO

FIGURE 7.2
1–1 Mapping

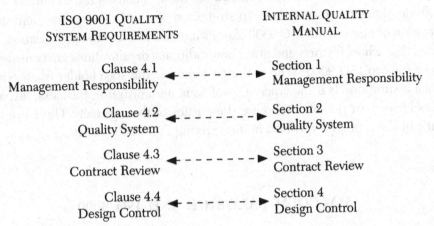

ISO 9001 QUALITY SYSTEM REQUIREMENTS	INTERNAL QUALITY MANUAL
Clause 4.1 Management Responsibility	Section 1 Management Responsibility
Clause 4.2 Quality System	Section 2 Quality System
Clause 4.3 Contract Review	Section 3 Contract Review
Clause 4.4 Design Control	Section 4 Design Control

9000 document are to be interpreted for its specific operations. The auditor ensures that the specific clause is addressed, quality documentation exists, and operations are consistent with the documentation.

ISO 9001 INTERPRETATION

This book presents a general process or methodology for becoming registered. For specifics on interpreting ISO 9001/9002/9003, investigate some of the excellent "what is" ISO 9000 books on the market.

Interpretation of a quality system requirement or a specific clause is usually based on context—on who is doing the interpreting and how it is implemented. ISO 9001 requirements are broad and allow for different interpretations in different applications. This is the standard's greatest benefit but could be its greatest flaw. The standard was written broadly so that it could be applied in many industries and services. But it also is open to interpretation by the user, customer, auditor, and other stakeholders.

For example, under "contract review," Section 4.3.1, "the supplier shall establish and maintain documented procedures for contract review and for the coordination of these activities." First, what's a contract? Is it a purchase order, contract, customer-supplier certification, phone order, verbal order, request for proposal, or request for quotation? A contract may well be any and all of these. A contract generically is an agreement among two or more parties. It can be verbal or written. According to the Uniform Commercial Code, additional issues must be considered. But under ISO 9001, any of these is considered a contract.

Some organizations may have to stretch on some of these points, and interpretation of many of the ISO 9000 clauses must be fitted to the organization. I've heard that school districts and other nontraditional organizations are considering registering to ISO 9000. Who is the customer or the stakeholder in an educational institution? Is it the student, professor, administrator, business, taxpayer, school board, or parents? Who are the parties of the contract? These are only some of the problems involved in interpreting ISO 9000 clauses.

MALCOLM BALDRIGE AND ISO 9000

Many companies that are pursuing the Malcolm Baldrige National Quality Award (MBNQA) don't know what to do with ISO 9000. They seem to have to choose between two competing approaches to the quality issue.

There are clear distinctions between the two, however. The Malcolm Baldrige National Quality Award is an award or prize for world-class quality. ISO 9000 is a lowest-common-denominator, customer-supplier contractual hurdle. MBNQA is exclusive, and ISO 9000 is inclusive. Although there are other differences, there are similarities. Both focus on quality systems, control, and assurance. ISO 9000 is more internal, documentation, and control driven. ISO 9000 implementation, regardless of registration, is an excellent platform for developing quality systems, structure, and improvement. For this reason, many companies are adopting ISO 9000 quality systems and adapting them to their organizational structure.

FLOWCHARTING THE CURRENT QUALITY PROCESSES AND SYSTEMS

Modern industrial problems often cannot be solved on a piecemeal basis. Solutions involve interrelated, multidisciplinary systems that explore how processes really operate and then develop integrated problem-solving and training approaches.

THE IMPORTANCE OF UNDERSTANDING EXISTING SYSTEMS

In many organizations, operational systems and processes haven't been changed since they were initially installed. Problems simply are accepted by the organization. If something goes wrong, it is fixed. As Deming once said, 85 percent of business problems are the result of an organizational structure that results in systemic or chronic problems.

The easiest and most revealing method of understanding existing systems is to determine the cause of discrepancies or find the location of high costs. Deficiencies result in recalls, rework, scrap, lost time, lost productivity, and inevitably unhappy customers and lost revenues. At worst, a death or a major recall can jeopardize the operations or the future of a company.

Mistakes are made for a number of reasons: a task may be difficult or may not have been explained properly. Good operational performance requires consistency, which leads to uniform, high-quality products. Variation—the lack of consistency—usually creates many deficiencies. Variation can have many causes. New employees are insufficiently trained. Training is conducted differently among plants, shifts, and trainers. Procedures are different among plants. Procedures and policies are misunderstood.

FLOWCHARTING

One method for determining "what is" the current system in your organization is to create a flow chart or map of the processes. Flowcharting or mapping processes show how work, resources, material, people, or monies flow. Often, employees can assist or even map out the critical process steps since they already know the intricate workings of the process. Teams of workers may be capable of handling the mapping project from start to finish, instead of just mapping out one area.

Process flowcharting can

- Show how resources are used,

- Show how material is used,

- Show how value is added at each process step,

- Show where costs are added,

- Reveal inefficiencies,

- Reveal stoppages or deadlocks,

- Determine inspection or hold points,

- Assign responsibilities, and

- Identify process steps for critical product characteristics.

What processes can be mapped? Just about anything can be mapped, including resources, money, materials, patients, or people. Let me illustrate. Products are assembled in a manufacturing operation through a multitude of steps. Raw material may be machined into a finished product. Patients go through a hospital system from admitting to surgery to going home.

Figure 7.3 shows a flowchart of the process of auditing suppliers. ISO 9001 specifies under the "verification of purchased product" quality system requirement that if required by contract, the purchaser has the right to verify at the source that purchased products conform to contract requirements. The audit process flowchart shown in the figure starts with informing the supplier of the impending audit and continues with verifying corrective actions.

Processes share certain characteristics. Each consists of a number of discrete process steps. Each process step has inputs and outputs that form the inputs to the next step, and at each process step, value is added. Once the activities and measurements for each stage of the process have been defined, documented, and flowcharted, the ISO 9000 team can collect data on costs, waiting times, deficiency levels, and other quality information to reengineer and to proceduralize the process.

The following is a simple model for flowcharting a quality system:

- Determine the purpose of the process.

- Identify the process steps.

- Identify the value added in each process step.

- Determine the inputs and outputs of each process step.

- Measure the cost and productivity in each step.

- Analyze and determine whether the process has to be changed.

- Benchmark the comparable process in best-in-class processes.

FIGURE 7.3
Example of Customer-Supplier Audit Process Flowchart

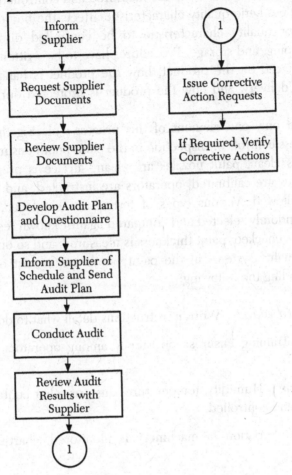

- Modify, if required, the existing process.

- Stabilize (control) processes.

- Write procedures describing how the work is conducted.

ANATOMY OF A QUALITY SYSTEM

The purpose and structure of a quality system may be understood in terms of the following manufacturing example. Marketing has determined that the customer wants specific product attributes, such as a "flawless" paint job. Engineers or plant personnel must define this customer quality requirement in terms of engineering specifications that can be measured and controlled on the production line. This cosmetic quality characteristic affects the buy decision and becomes a major quality characteristic to be controlled during production, handling, shipping, and storage. Procedures have to be written specifying how the paint is placed on the product, how the product is handled throughout production to delivery, and how the product is protected during storage and shipping.

Let's look at only one element of this process—placing the paint on the product. Process controls or inspection in the paint booth ensure that the paint environment is clean, paint nozzles are clean, surface is prepared properly, inspection gages are calibrated, operators are instructed, and procedures are consistently followed. Various types of testing are employed, as well. Paint samples are randomly selected and compared against known test samples. Surface adhesion is checked, paint thickness is measured, and so on.

ISO 9000 quality systems in the paint booth can consist of a number of elements, including the following:

- *Methods/procedures* Written instructions detail what to do when.

- *Training* Training ensures consistency among operators and departments.

- *Environment* Humidity, temperature, dust, or other contaminants are measured and controlled.

- *Machinery* Variation in machinery is monitored, charted, and controlled.

The goal of these quality system controls is to monitor and control process variation. This classical statistical control approach emphasizes stabilizing operations, maintaining control, and establishing capability and then improving them. Again, the goal is to ensure uniformity and consistency through documented proceduralization.

When analyzing existing quality systems or establishing the internal baselines to determine the current state of quality, the following should be examined:

- Level of internal deficiencies in existing system,

- Types of monitoring and control systems,

- Types of corrective action and their effectiveness,

- Compliance of the existing system with ISO 9000 requirements,

- Examination of implementing alternate quality systems,

- Determination of the cost of implementing alternate systems,

- Identification of human resources to support the quality system, and

- Level of upstream and downstream satisfaction with quality systems.

A challenge for many organizations is to integrate existing control systems with those of ISO 9001/9002/9003. The issue involves whether to improve and integrate older systems or to standardize on a newer system that can be a platform to easier integration and expansion. For many, the new platform for quality systems is Malcolm Baldrige or ISO 9000 criteria.

A fine balance has to be maintained between proceduralizing processes and maintaining flexibility. The goal is to develop current, complete, and useful instructions. Employees must trust management to empower them with the authority and responsibility to direct and manage their work. Procedures will be developed and followed as long as they are realistic and improve the quality of work life as well as the quality of products produced.

CONDUCTING THE ISO 9000 PREASSESSMENT

The preassessment is an internal audit of your operations. Technically, an internal quality audit is "a systematic examination of the acts and decisions by people with respect to quality, in order to independently verify or evaluate and report compliance to the operational requirements of the quality program or the specification or contract requirements of the product or service."[3]

The preassessment determines what "shall be" as required by ISO 9001/9002/9003 and "what is" in terms of quality systems documentation and process. In the ISO 9000 registration process, this is sometimes called *gap analysis* or *ISO 9000 readiness audit*. This evaluation process will assist you in understanding what is currently occurring in your operation. Internal auditing also satisfies a significant quality system requirement—having an independent and objective review function of your operations. (See Figure 7.4.)

Most quality audits, whether internal or for ISO 9000 registration, are based on verifying, evaluating, and reporting compliance or conformance to quality-related documentation. An audit examines the following:

- Organization goals and commitment are compared to the quality manual.

- Quality systems are compared against quality standards and procedures.

- Processes are compared against procedures and work standards or instructions.

- Products are tested and inspected against engineering specifications.

The registrar can conduct the audit as part of the registration contract, or you or an external consultant can conduct the preassessment. These are your operations, so you should remain closely involved with the preassessment. Often, ISO 9000 registration team members conduct the internal preassessment in their own functional areas. Instead of using the preassessment as a top-down means to monitor, assess, and evaluate operations, quality auditing may be used to evaluate operations by peer-level groups. For example, one area of manufacturing may quality audit upstream and downstream processes, areas, or steps.

If you don't have an internal quality audit system, then preassessment can serve as the basis for establishing one. A quality audit provides an objective and independent assessment and also can help you solve operational quality problems. Quality auditors can be used to

- Help solve other people's problems,

- Provide independent and objective evaluations,

- Serve as an agent of change, and

- Help educate personnel in quality techniques.

INTERPRETING ISO 9001/9002/9003

ISO 9000 quality systems auditors assess quality systems based on ISO 9001/9002/9003 requirements. This is not a simple process. The auditors know the intent and the concepts of the standard, but these must be interpreted in

FIGURE 7.4
Gap Analysis

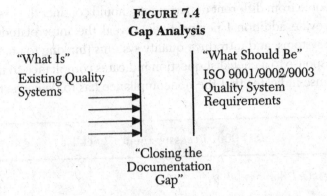

"What Is"
Existing Quality
Systems

"What Should Be"
ISO 9001/9002/9003
Quality System
Requirements

"Closing the
Documentation
Gap"

terms of the auditee's specific quality systems and process. The following examples illustrate the challenges confronting auditors.

Under Section 4.1.1 of ISO 9001, "quality policy," states that "The supplier's management shall define and document its policy and objectives for, and commitment to, quality." This is a simple, straightforward statement. But from the ISO 9000 quality auditors point of view, it raises several questions:

- Who is management? Is it the chief executive officer, chief operating officer, or the chief quality officer?

- What does "define and document" mean? Should the policy be included in the quality manual?

- What should the auditor do in the case of multiple locations?

- What are proper policy, objectives, and commitment statements?

- What should the company do if offshore operations operate under different customs and observe different customer requirements?

USING THE CHECKLIST

The sample checklist on pages 118–127 is one that the registrar's auditor uses in conducting the audit. Use this checklist to conduct your own internal ISO 9000 preassessment. If you follow the checklist, you'll determine what you need to do in terms of developing specific procedures and other quality documentation as specified by ISO 9001.

Several people from different departments should conduct the preassessment. They can provide additional perspectives, reveal the interrelatedness of ISO 9000 quality systems, and introduce quality systems thinking to an organization.

A "yes" response to a checklist question indicates compliance to the question. A "no" response indicates that the noncompliance has to be corrected.

ISO 9001 Preassessment Checklist

1. *Management Responsibility*

   Is top management actively involved in quality?

   Are quality policies, objectives, and plans developed?

   Are quality policies, objectives, and plans understood by employees?

   Are quality responsibilities and authorities defined for all personnel?

   Are specific employees responsible for and do they have the authority to conduct the quality activities, including

   a. Problem identification,

   b. Defect prevention,

   c. Correcting problems, and

   d. Ongoing operational control?

   Are internal resources allocated and dedicated for quality assessment, design reviews, inspection, and testing?

   Are assessment personnel objective and independent of those whose products are assessed?

   Has a management representative been appointed to be responsible for quality and ISO 9000?

   Are quality systems periodically evaluated for effectiveness and continued compliance?

   Are sufficient records maintained of organization and management quality activities?

(*continued on next page*)

ISO 9001 Preassessment Checklist (*continued*)

2. *Quality System*

Are quality systems maintained for ensuring that products conform to requirements?

Are all quality systems properly documented?

Does the quality documentation system include policies, procedures, plans, and work instructions?

Is documentation complete, current, and accurate?

Are quality policies accumulated in a quality manual?

Are quality plans prepared?

Do quality plans address the following:

a. Identification of quality controls,

b. Production compatibility,

c. Updating testing procedures,

d. Identification of measurement requirements,

e. Clarification of process and product requirements, and

f. Preparation of quality records?

3. *Contract Review*

Are contracts reviewed for capability, compliance, and special requirements?

Are customer requirements fully defined?

Are customer requirements fully understood?

Are differences between customer and supplier resolved?

Are contract modifications reviewed?

Are contract and customer requirements records maintained?

(*continued on next page*)

ISO 9001 Preassessment Checklist (*continued*)

4. *Design Control*

Are procedures developed to control and verify product design?

Does the design satisfy customer requirements?

Are plans developed to identify accountability and authority for development of the design?

Are design plans checked and updated throughout the product development cycle?

Is the design periodically checked and otherwise verified by qualified personnel?

Are technical, organizational, and other interfaces identified?

Are design input, output, and verification requirements identified?

Are design conflicts resolved effectively?

Does design output satisfy input requirements?

Are there reference or benchmark criteria for design input and output?

Are reference and benchmark criteria satisfied?

Are designs checked for regulatory or governmental compliance?

Are criteria and major product characteristics identified?

Are designs verified by competent and independent personnel?

Are calculations checked?

Are qualification tests conducted?

Are design changes verified and approved?

Is there sufficient documentation for controlling design and design modifications?

(*continued on next page*)

ISO 9001 Preassessment Checklist (*continued*)

5. *Document and Data Control*

Are design- and quality-related documents controlled?

Are documents reviewed and approved by authorized personnel?

Are quality documents available to appropriate parties?

Are obsolete documents removed from use?

Is there a master list of approved documents?

Is the master list accurate and up to date?

Is there an approved distribution list for documents?

Are changes to documents reviewed and approved by the same personnel initiating the documents?

Are changes to designs and documents properly reviewed?

Are changes identified on engineering drawings?

Is there a master list for controlling documents?

Are documents reissued after changes have been made?

6. *Purchasing*

Are purchased products assessed and monitored for compliance to requirements?

Are suppliers evaluated and monitored over the life of the project?

Are supplier records current, complete, and accurate?

Are quality system controls for purchased materials effective and efficient?

Are customer purchasing documents complete and understandable?

Are products fully described and identified?

Are purchasing documents periodically reviewed and approved by authorized personnel?

Can the customer verify the quality of purchased products through on-site audits?

(continued on next page)

ISO 9001 Preassessment Checklist (*continued*)

Do suppliers understand customer requirements?

Do supplier's suppliers understand customer requirements?

7. *Control of Customer-Supplied Products*

Does the supplier provide documentation of the verification, storage, and maintenance of customer-supplied products?

Is there sufficient documentation—a paper trail—identifying the quality of customer-supplied products?

8. *Product Identification and Traceability*

Are products identified and traceable throughout the production, delivery, and installation process?

Are products traceable by specific batches or lots?

9. *Process Control*

Are critical quality processes in control and capable?

Are the concepts of control, capability, and improvement understood?

Are critical and major quality areas clearly identified?

Do work instructions define key quality processes?

Are quality standards and reference documents identified?

Are key product quality characteristics identified?

Are key process variables relating to these quality product characteristics controlled?

Are processes and equipment approved by authorized personnel?

Are process and equipment changes approved by authorized personnel?

Are there workmanship instructions?

Are there special processes?

Are special processes certified?

(continued on next page)

ISO 9001 Preassessment Checklist (*continued*)

Are these special processes in control and capable?

Does documentation exist for normal and special processes?

10. *Inspection and Testing*

Are incoming products tested and inspected?

Are there other forms of certification?

Does inspection or verification follow a quality plan?

Are inspection and testing results properly identified and recorded?

Is receiving inspection and testing evaluated for effectiveness?

Are incoming inspection requirements related to the supplier's capability?

If a recall is required, can all products be retrieved?

Are in-process testing and inspection conducted?

Do in-process testing and inspection follow a plan?

Are major processes controlled and monitored?

Are major processes in control, capable, and improving?

Are products segregated until testing have been completed?

Are nonconforming materials properly identified?

Are there final inspection and testing?

Do final inspection and testing follow a quality plan?

Are products tested for conformance to customer requirements?

Are records maintained about test and inspection status and results?

11. *Control of Inspection, Measuring, and Test Equipment*

Are inspection, measurement, and test equipment controlled and calibrated?

Are the testing and measurement equipment capable of performing required measurements?

(*continued on next page*)

ISO 9001 Preassessment Checklist (*continued*)

Are the reliability and repeatability of the measurement equipment known?

Are the type of measurements specified?

Are the accuracy and precision of the instruments specified?

Are test and measurement equipment calibrated at prescribed intervals?

Are test and measurement equipment calibrated traceable to national standards?

If there are no national or international standards, is the rationale for calibration defined?

Do procedures specify the location, identification, acceptance criteria, frequency of verification, and type of verification of test and measurement equipment?

Is calibration status positively identified?

Are calibration records maintained for inspection, measurement, and test equipment?

Are inspection and measurements periodically assessed for accuracy?

Are environmental conditions suitable for accurate test and measurement?

Are handling and storage of test and measurement equipment specified?

Are test hardware and software calibrated?

Are test hardware and software capable of accurate and precise measurements?

Are inspection and measurement records up to date and accurate?

12. *Inspection and Test Status*

Are inspection and test status identified through tags or labels?

Are products positively identified for their inspection and test status?

Is identification maintained throughout product and installation of the product?

Does documentation record responsibility and authority to release products?

(*continued on next page*)

ISO 9001 Preassessment Checklist (*continued*)

---

13. *Control of Nonconforming Product*

    Are procedures established for ensuring that nonconforming products are not used or installed?

    Have nonconforming products been released and used?

    Are nonconforming products identified, documented, evaluated, segregated, and disposed of properly?

    Are all parties informed about nonconforming products?

    Are authority and responsibility for determining and disposing of nonconforming products defined?

    Are nonconforming products reviewed according to procedures?

    Are rework, acceptance, rejection, and regrade of products specified?

    Are nonconforming products ever used?

    Are procedures developed and followed for the use of nonconforming products?

    Are reworked or repaired products reinspected according to procedures?

14. *Corrective and Preventive Action*

    Are corrective action procedures developed and consistently followed?

    Are the symptoms and causes of nonconforming products determined?

    Are the symptoms and causes of nonconforming products eliminated?

    Are processes and reports investigated for determining patterns of failure?

    Are internal controls implemented after corrective action to ensure that problems don't recur?

    Are postaudits conducted to determine the effectiveness of corrective action?

    Are procedures rewritten to reflect changes due to corrective action?

(continued on next page)

ISO 9001 Preassessment Checklist (*continued*)

15. *Handling, Storage, Packaging, Preservation, and Delivery*

Are there procedures specifying proper handling, storage, packaging, and delivery?

Are there adequate means for handling materials?

Are products stored safely?

Are there adequate procedures for preventing damage or deterioration of products?

Are the conditions of products in inventory periodically evaluated?

Does packaging protect products?

16. *Control of Quality Records*

Are there procedures for identifying, collecting, and storing quality records?

Are quality documents and records accurate and current?

Are the records of suppliers and suppliers' suppliers accurate and current?

Are quality records accessible?

Are quality records retained for a sufficient amount time?

Are quality records available to the customer and other interested parties?

17. *Internal Quality Audits*

Are internal quality audits conducted?

Are internal quality audits properly planned, conducted, and reported?

Are audits prioritized?

Is there corrective action as a result of the audits?

Is corrective action effectiveness monitored?

Does top management review the effectiveness of corrective action?

18. *Training*

Are training needs identified?

(*continued on next page*)

ISO 9001 Preassessment Checklist (*continued*)

Are training resources adequate for the internal training needs?

Are all personnel trained in quality technologies?

Are training records maintained?

19. *Servicing*

Are there service requirements in the contract?

Are contractual service requirements complied with?

Are there procedures for satisfying and verifying contractual requirements?

20. *Statistical Techniques*

Are statistical techniques used in the organization?

Are statistical techniques used for determining production control, capability, and improvement?

Is statistical process control used?

CORRECTIVE ACTIONS

Deficiencies and discrepancies will be uncovered during the internal assessment. A deficiency is an instance or example of a specific ISO 9001/9002/9003 requirement that has not been satisfied. If you have a formal corrective action system, then issue a corrective action request (CAR) to fix the problem or eliminate the root cause. Again, this preassessment is what the registrar's auditor team will be doing during its assessment. The more your quality systems comply with ISO 9001/9002/9003, the less it'll cost you in the long run.

Two examples of CARs are presented in this book's appendix. While different, the basic elements of all corrective action are fairly straightforward:

- *Deficiency level* Is it a critical, major, or minor deficiency?

- *Location of the deficiency* Where is the deficiency located, and how prevalent is it?

- *Symptom and root-cause analysis*   How was the deficiency revealed, and what is a preliminary cause of the deficiency?

- *Effect on system or operation*   How does the deficiency affect operations or quality, including schedule, processes, product, and profitability?

- *Action taken or recommended*   What can or should be done to eliminate the symptom and the root cause of the deficiency?

- *Subsequent monitoring of corrective action*   Is the deficiency sufficiently critical that a reaudit is required?

When the registrar's auditors conduct their assessment, they will issue deficiency findings or corrective actions. They are similar to the above analysis. The difference is that their auditors will identify the ISO 9000 clause that indicates noncompliance. The auditors also won't conduct symptom or root-cause analysis, identify effects on your quality system, or recommend actions to correct the deficiency. It's your quality system, and it's up to you to find the correction.

COMMONSENSE RULES FOR RUNNING A BUSINESS

The preassessment process doesn't require superhuman endurance or world-class resources—just common sense. Understand your present quality systems and operations. Understand ISO 9001/9002/9003 requirements. Then close the gap between the two.

ISO 9000 is a foundation set of quality standards representing generally approved management principles. They are commonsense ways of running almost any business. ISO 9001/9002/9003 are a family of internal quality system controls that are documentation based. The documentation, policies, procedures, and instructions detail who does what and where.

As long as these controls are in place, deficiencies are prevented from occurring. If, however, they do occur, then corrective actions should be able to correct the problem and prevent the recurrence. Periodic internal auditing also should be able to identify problems before they occur. The goal of the entire system of controls is to correct problems and prevent them from recurring.

In the next Step, we discuss how to develop quality documentation.

Percentages of ISO 9001 Discrepancies

The most commonly occurring discrepancies are listed below. Document control quality system discrepancies or deficiencies occur most often. Many companies are averse to documenting procedures and proceduralizing operations.

Section Number	Title	Percent Nonconforming
4.5	Document Control	18%
4.4	Design Control	12
4.6	Purchasing	9
4.10	Inspection/Testing	8
4.2	Quality System	7
4.9	Process Control	6
4.11	Inspection/Measuring/Test Equipment	6
4.3	Contract Review	5
4.14	Corrective and Preventive Action	4
4.1	Management Responsibility	4
4.16	Quality Records	4
4.15	Handling/Storage/Packaging/Delivery	4
4.17	Internal Quality Records	4
4.18	Training	3
4.12	Inspection/Test Status	2
4.13	Control of Nonconforming Product	2
4.8	Product Identification/Traceability	2
4.19	Servicing	0
4.20	Statistical Techniques	0
4.7	Customer-Supplied Products	0

STEP 8

DEVELOP QUALITY DOCUMENTATION

Key Steps
• Document and proceduralize ISO 9000-required quality systems and processes.
• Determine which non-ISO 9000-specified systems and processes to proceduralize and document.
• Determine who develops what quality documentation.
• Understand the different levels of quality documentation.
• Map and number quality documentation to the ISO 9000 requirements.
• Write simple, understandable, and usable policies, procedures, and work instructions.
• Control distribution and approvals of quality documentation.

Following the preassessment, you'll know where your quality systems are weak and where you need to develop quality documentation. The basic purpose of the documentation is to communicate intentions, information, data, decisions, commitment, specifications, policies, or instructions.

PROCEDURALIZATION

ISO 9000 registration can affect an organization's operations and quality systems. If a company has a longstanding quality program, however, it will have quality systems, proceduralized operations, stabilized processes, and documented controls in place throughout the organization. If quality procedures already exist, the only major changes are to harmonize existing quality systems to ISO 9000. This may require only establishing a new documentation format or renumbering existing procedures and work instructions.

What about the organization that does not have documented quality systems? In these organizations, ISO 9000 registration is more difficult because ISO 9000 quality systems must be designed, implemented, and documented from the top down. This is a time-consuming process and particularly difficult in organizations where the value of quality systems is not understood. A quality manual, policies, specifications, procedures, and work instructions have to be developed.

PROCEDURALIZING OPERATIONS

At this stage of the registration process, ISO 9000 quality systems and practices should be carefully defined and proceduralized. ISO 9000 systems thinking and implementing should become part of the normal business environment and operating practices. It's not always easy to integrate these practices into the organization's way of doing business. Procedures and work instructions must be written, and people must be trained in the procedures. Over time, the procedures become institutionalized or operationalized into the organization and are considered part of normal operations or good business.

Proceduralization is also a basic tenet of quality control. As long as work is conducted in a uniform and consistent manner and detailed in quality documentation, then the outputs of these actions should satisfy customers. The goal of quality control is to determine what internal or external customers want and to develop process specifications satisfying these requirements. If internal activities consistently follow these procedures, then the process should be controlled and stabilized. Workers or teams monitor a process. If the process goes out of control, then workers or teams can determine the cause, eliminate it, and adjust the process back into control. Fixing and eliminating the root cause is the rationale behind corrective action. The long-term goal is to limit process variation through proceduralization, monitoring, correction, prevention, and improvement.

Again, consistency and uniformity are the hallmarks of quality. Work instructions are important in process control. The instructions direct production personnel at various levels of the organization on how to control the process. Directions ensure uniformity of understanding, performance, and control. If system variation should occur, such as personnel changes, the documentation serves as the main method for controlling variations caused by different personnel and methods.

PROCEDURALIZING NONSPECIFIED ACTIVITIES

ISO 9001/9002/9003 require that specific quality-related activities be documented and controlled. However, an organization involves other important value-adding activities not addressed in these documents, such as finance, administration, and accounting processes.

Should activities not specified or required by ISO 9001 be proceduralized? The simple answer is that for ISO 9000 compliance, the activity doesn't have to be proceduralized. However, if the purpose is to improve operations through consistency, then all critical operations should be proceduralized, documented, and made uniform. It doesn't make sense to have only some processes and systems improve and not others. All operations in an organization should add value, both internally and externally. Process steps in the process chain not adding value should be eliminated. Process elements that add value but can become unstable should be proceduralized.

PROCEDURALIZATION IN DIFFERENT
ORGANIZATIONAL ENVIRONMENTS

ISO 9000 quality systems must be tailored to the organization—to its culture, people, processes, and products. Employees must accept and feel comfortable using ISO 9000 quality systems. The goal is eventually to integrate the quality system at the working daily level so that there is a seamless quality system process specifying and documenting work, information, and other resource flows. This doesn't happen quickly.

ISO 9000 proceduralization can be difficult in an authoritarian structure. Proceduralization imposed on an organization can result in reactions ranging from indifference to resistance. Employees may see ISO 9000 proceduralization as a management control mechanism for enforcing rules and establishing operational order. In a worst case, employees may see proceduralization as a reengineering process for downsizing the organization and may attempt to sabotage the registration initiative.

ISO 9000 registration and proceduralization require a commitment by all employees to establish effective quality systems that satisfy downstream and inevitably final customers. The best and perhaps the only way to do this is for employees who actually perform the tasks to assist in writing the procedures. Developing and implementing quality systems may become a slow and incremental approach that solicits input, develops the procedure, reviews it, and revises it. The hoped-for result is developing procedures that reflect how work is efficiently conducted.

Why should workers or functional teams support the ISO 9000 initiative? This is a "What's in it for me?" type of question. If employees assist or preferably develop the procedures, then they should feel some ownership of the systems, especially if they improve the quality of work life. When procedures are understood, accepted, and developed by those in the work area, the quality systems have a much better chance of becoming accepted. Systems may be developed that make the work place safer, work more challenging, and the work environment more stimulating. All of this leads to recognition of performance, growth potential, and job stability. This process is easier in a rewarding and respectful professional environment than in a low-paying service environment.

TYPES OF DOCUMENTATION

When it comes to developing quality, less is more and less is better. Quality documentation should be simple and usable.

Quality documentation is commonly structured in terms of the following:

- Level I documentation,

- Level II documentation,

- Level III documentation, and

- Level IV documentation. (See Figure 8.1.)

FIGURE 8.1
ISO 9000 Documentation Pyramid

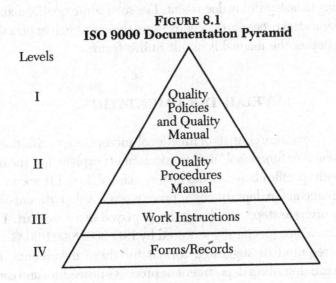

Levels

I · Quality Policies and Quality Manual

II · Quality Procedures Manual

III · Work Instructions

IV · Forms/Records

LEVEL I DOCUMENTATION

Level I documentation, the quality manual, responds to particular ISO 9000 requirements. In other words, the auditor, during the preassessment or during the audit, will check the manual to ensure that all pertinent ISO 9000 clauses are covered. The auditor can assess the system much easier if the manual uses the structure and numbering of the ISO 9000 quality standard.

The quality manual outlines quality policies dealing with ISO 9000 implementation, registration, and maintenance. The quality manual is just what it says it is. It deals with quality issues surrounding the management, assurance, and control of quality. It doesn't deal with the other important issues surrounding selling, marketing, designing, producing, sourcing, and delivering products. The "what is" and "how to" of these functional areas are found in departmental procedures manuals. The appendix to this book has copies of a generic quality manual, procedures, and work instructions.

Large, multisite organizations will have a companywide quality manual. Each division, business unit, and plant may have quality manuals that echo the companywide quality manual. They are similar in vision, mission, and structure. Why? Each business unit, regardless of its products, must comply with the intent and purpose of ISO 9000. That's why most quality manuals follow a standardized format.

Some companies have incorporated operational procedures into their quality manual, resulting in an unwieldy document. I've seen some quality manuals that incorporate operational procedures occupy more than twenty feet on a shelf. It is questionable whether the manual is usable in this form.

LEVEL II DOCUMENTATION

Second-tier documentation consists of functional and/or area specific documents. These departmental or functional "how to" documents explain how the organization complies with specific clauses in the quality manual. Level II documentation normally is prepared at the department or process level. A department or process may have many discrete steps, which may be displayed in a flowchart. This level of documentation is not specifically required by ISO 9001/9002/9003.

There is no required or suggested format for these documents. Level II documentation can describe a department or process's procedure and can be one to six pages long. The three examples and formats of internal quality audits, corrective action requests, and introductory quality training procedures are shown in the appendix on pages 197–198, 199, and 200–201.

Examples of Level II documentation include

- Customer service training,

- Service installation and maintenance,

- Quality auditing procedures,

- Purchasing procedures, and

- Quality inspection procedures.

LEVEL III DOCUMENTATION

Level III documentation explains how work is actually done. Level III documentation details "how to" inspect products, run a computer lathe, or assemble a telephone. It provides sufficient detail so that a new person can do the job and maintain quality.

Should all organizational systems be documented? Again, detailing every process step or work area in an organization isn't required by ISO 9000. The registrar's auditor won't assess these steps; the auditor assesses compliance to specific ISO 9000 clauses. Some functional areas aren't addressed in ISO 9001/9002/9003, including marketing, finance, customer service, and accounting. However, if these functional areas involve the control of quality, then consider developing procedures and work instructions.

Examples of this level of documentation include

- Product testing procedures,

- Statistical sampling procedures,

- Internal audit checklists,

- Laboratory procedures, and

- Calibration procedures.

LEVEL IV DOCUMENTATION

Some companies have Level IV documentation, which includes quality forms and other forms for noting information. The user fills out the form—which may be on a computer or in written form—with the required information. The purpose of this level of documentation is to secure information in a structured manner so that it is available to users.

Examples of this level of documentation include

- Purchase orders,

- Sampling forms,

- Accept or reject forms,

- Statistical process controls charts,

- Calibration tags,

- Service tools and software,

- Spare parts lists, and

- Test certifications.

In the next section, we discuss how to develop ISO 9000 documentation.

HOW TO DEVELOP DOCUMENTATION

ISO 9000 quality policies are found in the quality manual and can vary from company to company. They must reflect the requirements of the specific ISO 9000 standard, however—either ISO 9001/9002/9003. Quality policies can fall within the broad outlines of the ISO 9000 standard. In general, quality policies should

- Reflect the intent and the requirements of the appropriate ISO 9000 standard,

- Reflect the organization's mission, vision, and values,

- Be usable,

- Be flexible and adaptable, and

- Be comprehensive and include the entire organization.

In this section, we'll discuss the following:

- How to develop a quality manual,

- How to develop and write quality procedures, and

- How to develop and write work instructions.

HOW TO DEVELOP A QUALITY MANUAL

A quality manual is a

- System of quality ISO 9000 policies and organizational quality procedures,

- Means of communicating rules, requirements, and expectations,

- Live document that is continuously changing,

- Proof of organizational and management quality commitment, and

- Foundation and umbrella quality document.

The quality manual should tell people who, what, when, where, and how—the essence of all instructions and procedures. Focus on these questions when writing policies, procedures, and instructions, providing directions, developing the ISO 9000 project plan, justifying resources, or communicating the purpose of ISO 9000 registration.

The quality manual describes

- *What* quality system elements are addressed,

- *What* the organizational policies are,

- *How* the policies are complied with, and

- *Who* is responsible for compliance.

To fully explain how to develop a quality manual would require an entire book. In fact, two-day workshops are conducted on how to write a quality manual. The appendix has a sample quality manual that complies with—and in some quality systems requirements surpasses—the latest ISO 9001 quality system requirements. This sample quality manual will give you some ideas on how to develop yours. Here are some further tips for developing your quality manual:

- Number the sections in your quality manual to correspond one to one with the numbering of the ISO 9001/9002/9003 quality system requirements (clauses).

- Date all pages.

- Distribute all pages to approved parties.

- Develop a master list of copies distributed to suppliers and customers.

- Record changes and modifications.

- Remove dated procedures.

- Reissue corrected procedures.

- Be general.

- Avoid specifics that can result in a corrective action request.

- Allow for changes.

- Be consistent.

- Allow the registrar to review changes to quality systems and manual.

- Creatively adopt from existing manuals.

HOW TO DEVELOP AND WRITE QUALITY PROCEDURES

Procedures are specific to a division, business unit, or plant. They describe the accepted procedures for functional areas in these stand-alone businesses. One quality manual may be used by a multisite organization that also has specific manuals of quality procedures for individual sites. The procedures describe how activities are conducted within the business unit. For example, the procedures for conducting inspections or ensuring traceability may vary among plants.

If you want to write your own procedures, use internal staff specialists, process personnel, and a facilitator. It's helpful to create a flowchart of critical quality systems, especially those involving second-tier documentation. For example, a design process flowchart may help the ISO 9000 quality auditing team as well as the internal auditors identify critical process steps across several departments.

In general, quality procedures answer the following questions:

- What is done? What work is covered by the procedure?

- Why is it done? Why is work performed in the manner it is?

- Who does it? Who is responsible?

- When is it done?

- Where is it done? Where is production or inspection conducted?

- What resources are required? What work is covered by the procedure?

The Two-Page Procedure or Work Instruction

Procedures and work instructions used to be based on U.S. military models. Often ten or more pages described every element of a process or work instruction. The procedures covered process inputs, process outputs, tests, personnel, training, testing, moving, handling, storing, machine equipment, test equipment, methods, sampling methods, inspection methods, materials, approval, distribution, supplemental documents, and so on.

This elaborate and time-consuming method of writing procedures provided too much detail and ancillary information—much more than was necessary to get the job done.

More and more organizations are generating two-page procedures and work instructions. The procedure is a series of cookbook steps leading to satisfied internal or external customers. Extraneous information is eliminated. The work instruction includes, for example, all the critical steps needed to get a job done. Instructions include

- Critical steps of operation, test, and maintenance,

- Instruments, gages, tools, or other equipment needed at each step,

- Critical process or product steps,

- Inspection or tests at critical points,

- Drawings such as a schematic of the finished part, a process flowchart of the steps, or other pictorial information,

- Time standards, and

- Special notes on the bottom of the page identifying
  —Tips,
  —Special instructions,
  —Exceptions, and
  —Do's or don'ts.

The two-page procedure sounds too simple to people educated in writing complex procedures. But it works. This simple procedure also can be used as part of a company's on-the-job training efforts.

HOW TO DEVELOP AND WRITE WORK INSTRUCTIONS

Work instructions are specific to a work area, process, or machine. These are sufficiently detailed to inform a worker how to perform a function so that products—the outputs—meet requirements.

Work instructions should

- Reflect the best methods of doing something,

- Reflect what is being done,

- Incorporate the input of experts as well as line personnel, and

- Comply with the intent and objectives of ISO 9000 requirements and of the organization.

The following how-to steps can help an internal team to develop or rewrite an existing work instruction or procedure to reflect what is done and the best way for doing it:

1. The worksite team develops and writes the work instruction.

2. The process expert, supervision, and other process stakeholders (upstream or downstream personnel) review the work instruction procedure.

3. People performing the work then review the instructions and follow the steps.

4. If workers follow the procedural steps and don't produce products or services that satisfy downstream customers, then repeat steps 2 and 3.

5. If workers can follow the steps in the instructions and produce quality products, then ask workers outside the work area to follow the steps in the work instruction and evaluate the work instruction. If those unfamiliar with the procedure can follow the instructions, then stop.

To ensure successful procedures and work instruction development, note these tips:

- Simplify, simplify, and simplify.

- Post procedures in the work area.

- Post drawings and other graphical information at eye level.

This process has several advantages:

- Employees develop and own their own procedures and work instructions.

- Teams solve problems.

- Experts and supervision have input into the process.

- Stakeholders such as upstream and downstream personnel have a chance to review procedures.

- The procedure process develops real-life documents that will be used.

WHO SHOULD DEVELOP QUALITY DOCUMENTATION?

Documentation development is the major cost of registration, especially for organizations that don't have extensive or any quality systems. Quality documentation can be developed in several ways:

- An external or internal consultant may be retained to write procedures.

- The site ISO 9000 team may write the procedures.

- The work area team and/or an individual from the work area may write the procedures.

Many functional groups develop procedures and work instructions affecting their work area. Paying consultants or staff to facilitate this effort is the largest part of the registration cost.

Writing quality documentation is a skill, and the down side to developing one's own quality documentation is that your staff may not have that skill. Many companies, especially medium and small companies, hire consultants to write quality ISO 9000 documentation. ISO 9000 documentation development varies in cost. Technical writing consultants with engineering degrees and extensive quality background will develop documentation reflecting your needs and requirements. But writing site- and process-specific procedures and work instructions is difficult for someone outside your organization. You have several options. The technical writer may develop generic quality documents or customize standard software documentation to fit your systems. Developing site-specific documentation will cost you more.

WHAT PROCEDURES AND WORK INSTRUCTIONS
SHOULD BE DOCUMENTED?

Where should the ISO 9000 team start in terms of developing first-, second-, and third-level documentation? Most quality manuals comply with specific ISO 9000 standards. It's more difficult to determine the procedures and work instructions that should be documented.

You don't have to document every function, activity, or task. The standards state under process control that documented procedures are necessary where "the absence of such procedures could adversely affect quality." What could adversely affect quality during production? Assembly, test, and inspection actions of production workers and teams definitely could affect quality. But should there be an instruction explaining how to drive a forklift? There may be a procedure if the forklift driver must comply with a safety regulation. But the critical question is whether operating the forklift and handling products affects product quality. If it does, then a procedure should be written. These are your decisions and should incorporate input from the lowest possible level—at the operator or work area team level.

Sometimes procedures and work instructions are not documented because employees have been doing the same work without an accident for a number of years. Supervision and management may think that everyone is doing the same thing the same way. Again, the goal is to minimize variation through consistent operations. The people who do the actual work should know the best way of doing the job.

The question will arise that if internal customers are satisfied, then why would procedures be necessary. Procedures should be used to document what is really done. It compells operators, process specialists, work place teams, and first-line supervisors to look at what is being done and to examine how it is being done. Are actions adding value? Can they be done better? Can some activities be eliminated? Can some activities be rearranged? As you can see, many issues surrounding developing procedures deal with reengineering, self-managed teams, and proceduralization.

The quality policy and procedures manuals are usually controlled documents which means their distribution is restricted to approved holders. Also, the quality documentation approvals and revisions are arranged carefully. These are discussed in the next section.

MAINTAINING AND MANAGING QUALITY DOCUMENTATION

Two key words and concepts found throughout ISO 9001/9002/9003 are that documentation will be "developed" and "maintained." "Developed" implies they exist. "Maintained" implies they are current, accurate, and complete.

CONTROLLING QUALITY DOCUMENTATION

ISO 9000 registration in a large organization with multiple sites increases the amount of information to be distributed and increases the burden on control. In many cases, the highest-level quality documentation—the quality manual—is common throughout the organization. Level 2 and level 3 documentation involve specific procedures and work instructions. These are tailored to the specific site, processes, quality systems, and products.

Often, quality documentation is divided into separate manuals. The quality manual is used throughout the entire organization. More specific plant documents are developed, written, and updated by site personnel. The quality department (or whoever develops and organizes quality documentation) maintains and updates the master documentation list.

Another means of controlling documentation is to have departments maintain their own documentation. For example, the engineering department deals with engineering prints, bills of material, technical specifications, and so on. The purchasing department maintains purchase orders, contracts, purchased material specifications, inspection reports, customer and supplier ratings, certification reports, and supplier audit results. The quality department maintains and updates audit results, test data, inspection reports, and all other quality documentation.

One problem that arises when documentation is shared and reviewed by many vertical and horizontal levels is that the result may be out of date. Another problem is unapproved revisions. To prevent document chaos, a central document repository or group often handles organizationwide documentation.

DOCUMENTATION APPROVALS

Quality policies, procedures, and work instructions go through an approval process. As a general rule, the higher the level of documentation and the broader the application or level of risk, then the higher the level of approval needed. Quality documentation approval follows the principle that area supervision and whoever else is affected should review and approve the document. Quality policies are reviewed and approved by top-level managers because they affect the entire organization. Procedures are approved by the area managers and by managers affected by the document.

In larger organizations, a corporate clearing group tracks and maintains quality documentation. This group has the overall organizational perspective, so quality documents dealing with safety, environmental, or regulatory affairs may require additional approvals.

The following is a list of tips for reviewing document approvals:

- Determine the appropriate level of review.

- Determine who should be involved in document review.

- Establish a single point of contact and management of document changes.

- Establish a board of departmental representatives to review changes.

- Develop procedures for reviewing quality documentation.

- Establish levels of quality documents and types of revisions.

- Establish controls for distribution of documentation.

- Establish procedures for reviewing the completeness, accuracy, and effectiveness of documents.

- Establish controls for expediting procedures.

ON-LINE DOCUMENTATION

Computerized on-line documentation can be used to maintain and revise quality documentation. A central corporate group often issues, tracks, and updates companywide documentation. This group may be part of engineering or quality assurance. It may control the master list of engineering prints, standards, specifications, bills of material, contracts, and other organizationwide documentation.

A centralized document control system works well in most circumstances, but problems can arise. The central control group may hinder product development or drawing changes or may not have adequate resources to deal with thousands of documents throughout the organization. The group may control access to documentation so that concurrent or simultaneous development projects don't grind to a halt.

A more democratic process for access is through computerized quality documentation. Computerized documentation allows users to

- Access information rapidly,

- Revise or update documentation, and

- Compare, collate, and analyze diverse information.

IT'S PEOPLE

ISO 9000 registration and implementation involve organizational systems and human factors more than machine technologies. Many software and quality products all but guarantee registration. These registration aids cannot be implemented successfully without quality beliefs, commitment, and action. Employees, especially those who maintain the quality systems after the registration audit, must believe in the power and benefits of quality system controls. The brief example on page 148 illustrates the problems that arise when technology is emphasized over people.

Software has been developed that can help you control and track the registration process, but it is only as good as the people using it. The software is an aid to the registration process. People must still organize, assess, plan, and manage the process.

In the next Step, we discuss how to select a registrar.

ISO 9000 Software Registration Aids

Software can help you become registered. Here are some examples of specific and generic software:

- *Auditing*   Auditing software consists of ISO 9000 checklists. Some software includes corrective action documentation and tips on how to correct problems.

- *Documentation*   ISO 9000 registration is documentation intensive. Documentation software offers generic quality manuals based on ISO 9001/9002/9003 criteria. Procedures and work instruction examples also are included. The off-the-shelf documentation usually has to be tailored to a specific operation.

- *Teams*   Team software is used for tracking people and projects. Team-building tools include brainstorming, check sheets, pareto analysis, and so on.

- *Project management*   Project management tools can be very sophisticated in tracking teams, resources, responsibilities, expenditures, and activities.

Is It Worth It?

Companies invested enormous amounts in technology in the 1980s. Has it been worth it? The answer is, "Maybe." Simple technology investments that target specific production or engineering problems and are easy to control do pay off. Unfortunately, many technology decisions were made by people who did not understand technology or its application within the company. Financial officers and engineers looked at projected benefits and costs to arrive at an investment decision. Unfortunately, staff members often didn't consult with the people using the technology and didn't understand how it would be used. They may have inflated benefits and underestimated costs.

Unfortunately, many technology investments did not include the operator—the person who had to monitor and control the process. As technical machinery was purchased, more technical staff, often process engineers, were hired to maintain the machinery. Production people became disillusioned because their responsibility was usurped by engineers.

SELECT A REGISTRAR

Key Steps
• Plan, prepare, and train extensively before the full audit.
• Conduct a preassessment audit and correct all deficiencies before the registrar's audit.
• Follow a structured process for selecting a registrar.
• Understand and itemize what the registrar will provide.
• Develop and prioritize selection criteria for selecting a registrar.
• Estimate the total costs (internal and external) of registration.
• Conduct a rough cost-benefit analysis.
• Pursue registration only if benefits exceed costs.
• Plan the audit jointly with the registrar.
• Remember that the registrar becomes your long-term partner.
• Understand the registrar's concerns and needs.
• Postpone or cancel a scheduled audit only if necessary.
• Understand why audits fail and develop contingencies.

There are more than thirty accredited registrars in the United States, including European, Canadian, and U.S. firms. Is there a best registrar or a group of superior registrars? Not really. Most accredited ISO 9000 registrars are competent; the marketplace is efficient in weeding out the unprofessional and disreputable. The bottom line is to talk to a half dozen or so registrars and see which ones seem to be the best fit. The following discussion should help put the selection issues in perspective.

WHAT DO CUSTOMERS WANT?

A recently conducted survey asked small businesses, "What are you looking for in a registrar?" The answers are revealing. When choosing a registrar, customers seem interested in the following:

- Accreditation,

- Full-time or part-time staff,

- Auditor knowledge,

- Scheduling,

- Objectivity and independence, and

- Costs.

ACCREDITATION

Registrars are certified or accredited by bodies that confirm that auditor and registration standards are followed. The main accreditor in the United States is the Registrar Accreditation Board (RAB). The private board assesses registrars in much the same manner as registrars audit companies. Once audited, the board offers its seal of approval. Europeans have similar boards that certify U.S. and European registrars. Most U.S. registrars carry the RAB and European seals of approval.

FULL-TIME OR PART-TIME STAFF

When ISO 9000 registration started in the United States, many registrars weren't sure there was enough business to hire full-time auditors and pay them benefits and salaries. Instead, they hired contractors to help conduct audits. When variation in auditor performance diluted the real and perceived quality of ISO 9000 registration, registrars began hiring full-time auditors to stringently ensure audit uniformity.

Companies pursuing registration want to deal with an auditing organization that is going to be around tomorrow. Ask your registrar for the number of their auditors who are full-time employees and for the background of their contractor auditors. Also ask for auditors' resumes.

AUDITOR KNOWLEDGE

Many ISO 9000 auditors learned their craft by conducting regulatory audits for regulatory compliance audits such as the U.S. Food and Drug Administration and the U.S. Department of Defense. Others learned their craft by conducting industry-specific commercial audits. ISO 9000 auditors may have to audit companies in different industry sectors. Ask potential registrars for their scope of registration, for references, and for their experience in conducting audits in your industry sector.

SCHEDULING

At the beginning of each year, registrars allocate auditors to scheduled audits. The registrar knows that existing registered companies need to have surveillance audits. It also tries to find new customers so that all its auditors are kept busy throughout the year conducting either registration or maintenance audits. The registrar will try to match the availability of auditors to customers. If a customer cancels an audit, it may have to wait months until there is another opening to conduct the audit. Some registrars have registration queues four or more months long. It's important to schedule realistic dates for your audit.

OBJECTIVITY AND INDEPENDENCE

A major problem with ISO 9000 registration is the appearance of (if not actual) conflict of interest when auditors are used for both consulting and auditing. From the registrar's point of view, its auditors have to be kept busy—whether through auditing, training, consulting, or providing other services. The registrar may require that the auditor who doesn't have any assessment business provide other revenue generating services, such as ISO 9000 consulting.

How can objectivity and independence be maintained if the consultant who advises a company on how to pass the audit also performs the audit for that company? The registration community has dealt with this issue in several ways.

Some registrars consult and conduct audits under the same organizational umbrella but separate the two functions. If both groups report to the same general management, however, this arrangement still provides the appearance of conflict of interest. Some registrars offer training but do not offer specific consulting. Some registrars partner with outside consulting firms. Registrars also emphasize that retaining and implementing the advice of the consultant doesn't ensure registration. Finally, the registrar may offer a half dozen choices of approved consultants.

How does a company—or the customer—who is relying on the registration know that there is total independence? The customer doesn't know. Ask the registrar for a position on this issue. Should you seek further verification, such as a written statement? Probably not. But ask your customer or whoever is requiring registration about the conflict-of-interest issue.

COSTS

The external cost of registration is fairly straightforward. All registrars charge comparable fees. The difficult cost to estimate is the internal cost.

Many companies think about the registration cost only when they want to pursue registration. Bids are solicited from registrars and compared, and the lowest or near to the lowest bid is chosen. But the internal cost of registration can be many times higher than the cost of the registrar. Why? Writing procedures and work instructions is a time-consuming task. If you don't have any, then preparing this documentation is a *very* time-consuming task.

Costs are such an important issue that they are discussed at length in the next section.

COSTING

You want to know how much ISO 9000 registration will cost. You've read the cost numbers in articles—$20,000 for a small company with internal costs of $100,000 or more. What's the truth? Again, the cost of registering and maintaining registrations is fairly straightforward, but the internal cost of becoming registered depends on a number of factors—basically, the existence, effectiveness, and documentation of quality systems. If you've got these and documentation is current, then the cost of preparing for registration will be much lower than if you must create complete internal quality systems.

It's impossible to estimate a realistic internal cost figure for the self-assessment and for developing quality documentation. Because the preassessment examines the difference between "what is" and "what shall be" according to the requirements of ISO 9000, the larger the difference, the costlier the preassessment. In addition, some costs are difficult to estimate, such as opportunity and risk-related costs.

Internal departments often have historical standards for costing out estimates for writing documentation, training, equipment down time, overhead, and other associated costs, but many variables just aren't known. How long will registration take? What will overhead rates or equipment utilization be over that period of time? Who will develop and write the procedures? How much training is required? The answers to these questions are also related to external factors that can't be predicted. Does the immediate customer or a further upstream customer want registration faster? What's the competition doing with ISO 9000 registration? Are you planning to sell products in regulated industry sectors or in countries requiring registration? Each of these can affect the internal cost of registration.

EXTERNAL COSTS OF REGISTRATION

The following factors affect registration costs:

- *Type of registration*   Because ISO 9001 involves all twenty quality systems requirements, it requires more audit time than ISO 9002 or ISO 9003.

- *Size of the organization*   The larger the organization, the more time it takes to audit the quality systems, processes, products, and people.

- *Type of processes and products*   Complex processes or products may require special testing or evaluation. The registrar may retain experts to conduct and assist in the audit.

- *Number of locations*   More locations require more observation and verification. This involves auditor and travel time, which adds costs.

Checklist of Internal Costs

The costs affecting your registration process include

- Registration costs,

- Preregistration assessment,

- Customer and competitive analysis,

- Internal labor rates,

- Consultants,

- Training,

- Equipment list (computers, copiers, and so on),

- Internal overhead,

- Management process review,

- ISO 9000 team,

- ISO 9000 team leader,

- Procedure writing, and

- Travel.

ADDITIONAL FEES TO DISCUSS WITH THE REGISTRAR

Most registrars charge comparable rates for auditing and registration services. Fees are listed in the registrar's application form. For several reasons, the registration fee structure usually is not negotiable: demand for registration exceeds the number of quality auditors and registrars; requirements for lead auditors are increasing; and customers are beginning to push the ISO 9000 registration requirements down to the supplier base.

Additional fees to discuss with the registrar includes the following:

- Application,

- Preregistration assessment,

- Quality documentation assessment,

- Annual registration,

- Periodic surveillance,

- Full recertification audit,

- Corrective action,

- Follow-up audits,

- Multiple-site audits,

- Offshore audits,

- Travel time,

- Analysis and report development,

- Postaudit corrective action analysis,

- Consulting services, and

- Ancillary services (mailing, copying, typing, faxing, and so on).

DAILY RATES

Here are the daily rates for various service providers:

- *Top ISO 9000 consultants* $1,500 and up. These people have extensive quality management backgrounds.

- *ISO 9000 implementation consultants* $750 to $1,250 per day. Implementation consultants help you organize, plan, and implement the program.

- *Document developers and writers* $60 to $125 per hour. Document developers write organization-, process-, and product-specific documentation to comply with ISO 9001/9002/9003 requirements.

- *Auditors* $1,250 to $1,750 per day. Higher rates are for specialized audits, such as for software.

- *Accreditation fee*   You may be interested in obtaining additional accreditation markets on your registration certificate. Each accreditation mark may cost up to $300 per mark per year.

Ballpark ISO 9001/9002 Registration Costs

ISO 9001

Company Size (number of employees)	Assessment (in thousands of dollars)	Surveillance Days Per Visit
1–30	$10.0	2
30–100	11.5	2
100–250	16.5	2
250–500	19.5	3
500–750	23.0	3
750–1,750	29.5	3
1,750–3,000	37.5	4
3,000–5,000	45.5	4

ISO 9002

Company Size (number of employees)	Assessment (in thousands of dollars)	Surveillance Days Per Visit
1–30	$ 8.0	2
30–100	10.0	2
100–250	11.5	2
250–500	16.5	2
500–750	19.5	2
750–1,750	23.0	3
1,750–3,000	28.0	3
3,000–5,000	36.0	3

Depending on the registrar, every three years you may have to reregister. This involves a total examination of all the ISO 9000 quality systems. If a company is ISO 9001 registered, then all twenty quality systems will be assessed based on the current ISO 9001 standard.

When estimating the total external cost of registration, base your estimate on the life cycle of registration. This includes the cost of becoming registered, cost of maintaining registration, cost of surveillance audits, and cost of recertification.

LOWEST OR BEST PRICE

Once you've received cost estimates from registrars, analyze the bids carefully. Should you take the lowest bid? Many companies do select registrars on the basis of the lowest bid.

Remember that a registrar may be monitoring or surveilling your facilities every six months or at least once a year. You want to work with a supplier that will help you improve your business. This partnering relationship may last many years.

Do you want to give your business to the lowest-price registrar? Resist this short-term thinking, and focus on marketing and positioning advantages, customer satisfaction, customer-supplier certification, or governmental compliance advantages provided by a registrar. Revisit the questions addressed in Steps 1 and 2, and determine which registrar can satisfy your needs the best.

A very low bid is difficult to dismiss. You may think you're getting a bargain. Remember, you are purchasing the credibility and reputation of the registrar. A registrar with an international reputation for excellence may charge up to 15 percent more than the average registrar and up to 40 percent more than the lowest bidder. You have to evaluate whether the higher-priced registrar is worth it.

The lowest bid may be suspicious for several reasons:

- The registrar didn't understand your requirements.

- The bid may be unrealistic and reflect the quality of auditing and registration.

- The bid may be for minimum services.

- The registrar may be new and require business to establish credibility.

- The bid may cover only registration and not ancillary costs.

IS IT WORTH IT?

The basic issue surrounding ISO 9000 registration is to determine its value to your organization. Once costs are estimated, they can be analyzed in terms of identifying personnel, acquiring money, dedicating time, allocating space, acquiring equipment, writing documentation, or obtaining consultants.

Estimating Challenges

Estimating the costs of registration is difficult. Various problems can arise during estimating, including the following:

• Misunderstanding what needs to be done,

• Overly optimistic schedule,

• Inaccurate work and time estimates,

• Improper internal skill sets,

• Internal obstacles and resistance,

• Unexpected changes,

• Not accounting for risks,

• Lack of management support,

• Lack of organizational support, and

• Lack of qualified resources.

Cost analysis is also an organizational reality check. Many companies want to pursue ISO 9000 registration without analyzing its costs and benefits. A company officer or executive may think that it's a neat idea and that the organization should just do it, but the hidden and internal costs can be high. Registration also may affect other programs, such as just-in-time, customer-supplier partnering, or reengineering implementation.

WORKING WITH THE REGISTRAR

At this point, you should be ready for the audit. You now understand the benefits and costs of registration. You've conducted the preassessment and gap analysis. You've closed the gaps by developing and documenting ISO-9000-specific quality systems. You're ready for the registrar's audit.

DEALING WITH THE AUDITORS

Work closely with the registrar. The registrar wants you to succeed as much or more than you do. Provide the registrar with all requested information. Depending on the size of your facility, two or more auditors will visit your facility. Try to understand what they have to contend with. Registrations are increasing yearly. Audit teams sometimes are on the road and away from their families for twelve or more days a month, including three weekends a month. A cross-country audit may require the auditor team to leave home on a Sunday to be at your plant early Monday morning. The work is long and tiresome. Audit reports are written in airports, planes, and hotels. The audit team will stress independence, objectivity, and professionalism, but auditors who seem that they just want to get the job done and go home can be unnerving to the auditee.

The following tips are useful for dealing with the audit team:

- *Be helpful and understanding.* The team wants to certify you almost as much as you want to be certified. But it has a job to do—to check your compliance to ISO 9001/9002/9003 standards. Auditors have questions to ask, policies and procedures to review, and quality systems to observe. Helping them do their job will get it done faster.

- *Answer all questions.* The auditors will follow their questionnaire, which is keyed to ISO 9001/9002/9003 requirements. They sometimes diverge from ISO 9000 requirements and ask peripheral questions to understand the full scope of the quality system.

- *Prepare for the audit.* The secret to a successful registration is planning. Ask your registrar what you need to provide for the audit.

- *Designate a person to assist the audit team.* Designate a lead person to provide the audit team with resources. This person may or may not shepherd the auditors, depending on whether the auditors feel that he or she will interfere with the assessment or compromise an auditor's honesty.

- *Provide on-site resources.* Inform everyone within the organization about the impending audit and what is required of each employee.

CANCELLING AN AUDIT

You may discover that additional procedures have to be written, key processes are out of control, and corrective actions have not been completed. The bottom line is that you're not ready. Consider the problems that your lack of preparedness causes for the registrar, who has planned and scheduled six months in advance to have three people at your site next week. The registrar may already have purchased tickets, made accommodations, rented a car, and so on.

Does this happen often? Yes. The registrar looks at a company seeking registration as a long-term partner. The registrar needs you as much as you need the registrar. The registrar will be surveillance auditing you every six months or every year for a long time to keep your name on the register. It truly is a long-term relationship.

What will the registrar do if you cancel several weeks before the audit? In most cases, the registrar will reschedule you, but you may have to go to the end of the queue again, which means postponing the audit for another six months or more.

What can you do to avoid these kinds of delays? The simple answer is to work with the registrar to ensure that everything's ready for the audit. A preassessment

---

Life of an Auditor

The life of an auditor is hectic. There's a lot of burnout. If the auditors leave home on a Sunday afternoon to make an early Monday audit, they check in late at a moderately priced hotel and review the customer's paperwork and other information. If the organization is large, a team of three auditors will conduct the two- to five-day audit.

The lead auditor has already planned the audit with his or her team. He or she has evaluated the quality manual and some other quality documentation. The lead assessor may determine, for example, that the registrar doesn't have specific expertise to evaluate a specialized chemical plant and request the assistance of a consulting specialist to explain technical process questions. Normally, the auditors have worked together on other assessments, and everyone knows his or her own responsibilities. The lead auditor conducts a final check of the plan to ensure that nothing unusual occurs at the auditee's site, and by the time the team arrives at your plant, they are ready to conduct the audit.

has been completed. Deficiencies have been corrected. Communications are good between the two of you. You're ready. Chances are good you'll pass on the first or second time through.

WORKING WITH THE AUDIT TEAM

The registrar's audit team assesses documentation and implementation compliance with the quality systems requirements of ISO 9001/9002/9003. Audit teams usually follow a consistent schedule.

STAGES IN THE AUDIT

The following is a typical chronological list of what the audit team will do at your facility:

- *Opening meeting*   The lead auditor explains the purpose, scope, and requirements of the audit to site management.

- *Quality manual assessment*   Your quality manual was sent to the registrar to do a preliminary compliance evaluation to the appropriate ISO 9000 standard, and during the audit a team member conducts a cursory check to determine whether you have made any changes to the manual. If the ISO 9000 standard has been revised, the auditor assesses whether the changes have been incorporated in the quality manual.

- *Previous corrective action requests (CARs)*   If the registrar is conducting a surveillance or a recertification audit and has issued previous CARs, the auditor evaluates the effectiveness of the registrant's actions to correct the CARs.

- *Internal audit and corrective actions evaluation*   During any surveillance audit, the audit team usually evaluates two critical quality system requirements—the registrant's internal audit and corrective action quality systems. Were internal quality systems periodically audited? Were corrective action requests issued? Were corrective actions implemented? Did problems recur?

- *Quality systems evaluation*   The audit team then assesses the implementation of all the quality systems as required by ISO 9001/9002/9003. The team assesses quality procedures and work instructions to ensure that system requirements are properly documented and implemented.

- *Deficiencies and corrective actions*   Deficiencies and noncompliance with the standards are noted. Corrective action requests are issued for critical, major, or minor deficiencies.

- *Closing meeting*   The lead auditor summarizes the findings to the site's top management, quality personnel, and others. A full audit report is issued within several weeks.

DISCREPANCY LEVELS

Registrars normally prioritize discrepancies by severity and issue CARs for documentation and implementation noncompliance. Some registrars use two levels to differentiate discrepancies; others use three levels:

- *Critical*   A critical discrepancy involves safety and health issues documentation or implementation noncompliances.

- *Major*   A major discrepancy may disrupt a process. It may indicate that no procedure currently covers the ISO 9001/9002/9003 requirement. There also may be multiple minor discrepancies or nonconformances in any one area which then become a major noncompliance.

- *Minor*   A minor discrepancy is a shortcoming in the documented quality system or an isolated example of nonconforming required practices.

Many registrars issue corrective actions for the critical and major system and process discrepancies. Minor discrepancies often can be fixed quickly. If the audit team discovers several minor discrepancies and the prospective registrant can correct them, then a CAR may not be issued.

If the auditor finds a critical or major discrepancy, then a corrective action request is issued requiring immediate attention and correction within a set period—often within thirty days. A critical or major discrepancy indicates a breakdown in internal control. Depending on the severity of the discrepancy, the registrar may require hard data or even independent verification of the effectiveness of the corrective action. The registrar may conduct a postcorrective action audit before issuing the registration certificate or before the next scheduled surveillance audit. When the company has corrected the deficiencies, it is issued a registration certificate.

Nonconformances, deficiency findings, or corrective action requests come in several forms. Two popular forms are illustrated here and on page 164. Their purpose is to indicate noncompliance or nonconformance to an ISO 9001/9002/9003 requirement. The nonconformance report has more narrative, while the corrective action request is more factual and formal.

Many companies don't pass their first registration audit. Why? Usually their documentation is deficient. In the next section, we offer simple tips for improving your registration chances.

Typical Nonconformance Report

1. Management responsibility for ensuring ISO 9001 compliance is confusing. Registrant has had three management representatives for ensuring compliance to the standard in the last six months. (Clause 4.1.2.3)

2. Internal audits are conducted yearly. Review of internal special processes indicates multiple out-of-control specifications. Internal audit of this area should be more frequent. (Clause 4.17)

3. Registrant reviews contracts only above $5,000. Each contract should be reviewed. (Clause 4.3)

4. The calibration report on the micrometer (instrument M-101) indicated an out-of-calibration condition. No report or corrective action was issued.

Typical ISO 9000 Auditor Noncompliance or Corrective Action Request

Customer or client:
Audit identification number:
Site location:
Date:
Lead auditor:
Customer representative:

For each noncompliance:
Noncompliance 1:
Critical/major/minor:
Reason:
ISO 9000 clause:
Area:

Noncompliance 2:
Critical/major/minor:
Reason:
ISO 9000 clause:
Area:

Noncompliance 3:
Critical/major/minor
Reason:
ISO 9000 clause:
Area:

Understood and accepted by customer:
Customer signature:

Corrective action follow-up:
Date corrected:

Verification/No verification:
Signature of lead auditor:
Signature of customer:

WHY REGISTRATION EFFORTS FAIL

Up to 50 percent of the companies audited do not pass the registration assessment on their first attempt. Why? The reasons vary. Perhaps the company did not understand the full requirements of registration and what was needed to pass the audit. Perhaps top management and others within the organization did not understand the requirement. Perhaps everyone thought it would be "a piece of cake."

If a company does not pass its first audit, it may try to assign blame. The ISO 9000 team leader and team may be accused of poor performance or ineffectiveness. Ultimately, the responsibility for ISO 9000 registration rests with senior management and the organization because the organization's quality systems documentation and implementation are being audited—not the team's effectiveness. Functional and work units also may be responsible for establishing, maintaining, and even documenting the quality systems.

Keep your expectations realistic. Keep informing the organization that corrective action requests are expected and are easily corrected. Constantly communicate with top management and the organization that ISO 9000 registration is doable but that sufficient resources and sufficient time must be allocated to do the task.

The final step is maintaining registration. Registration is not an end in itself. Although a major milestone in a continuous improvement journey, registration is but one goal among many.

Reasons That Registration Stalls

Registration is fairly straightforward. Given adequate time and resources, almost any organization can become registered. Why do some registrations take longer, spend more, have additional hurdles, or encounter resistance? Here are some of the reasons that registrations take longer or even stall:

- ISO 9000 goals and objectives are not understood.

- The ISO 9000 time objective is unrealistically short.

- Costs are underestimated.

- Internal communications are poor.

- Top management is not supportive.

- Staffing requirements are inaccurate.

- Internal operations support is insufficient.

- The registrant has planned poorly.

- The organization has poor internal morale.

- Project management tools are not used.

- Teams are not used.

- People are not working together.

- The audit consultant does not understand how to implement ISO 9000.

- The audit consultant is ineffective with ISO 9000 team.

- Policies, procedures, and work instructions are poorly written.

- The registrar queue (time to be registered) is long.

- Auditors are abrasive or unprofessional.

- The registrar doesn't communicate with the auditee.

STEP 10

MAINTAIN REGISTRATION

Key Steps
• Remember that your goal is continuous improvement: the journey doesn't stop at registration.
• Review ISO 9000 registration and implementation.
• Determine stakeholder satisfaction.
• Thank and recognize team members and others.
• Provide postregistration jobs for team members.
• Maintain quality systems.
• Establish an ISO 9000 maintenance team.
• Anticipate and prepare biyearly surveillance audits.
• Pursue continuous improvement.

ISO 9000 registration is a journey. It does not end when the registration certificate is issued. You are going to be audited every six months or once a year. You may have all your quality systems audited every three years to the appropriate standard—ISO 9001/9002/9003. The ISO 9000 standard itself is being rewritten every five years to incorporate new material. So once you implement and document quality systems, you need to maintain and improve them.

INTERNAL CLOSURE

Implementing ISO 9000 registration should not result in a full-time ISO 9000 bureaucracy. When registration is achieved, the ISO 9000 team normally disbands. Who then becomes responsible for registration maintenance activities? Now that quality systems have been operationalized, proceduralized, and documented, functional areas become responsible for their maintenance. One person or a corporate quality group may still be assigned to work and communicate with the registrar about ongoing corrective actions or scheduling issues. But the major part of the effort has been accomplished.

DISBANDING THE ISO 9000 REGISTRATION TEAM

ISO 9000 registration will not take forever. Full-time team members and leaders may wonder whether they still have jobs to return to. The following suggestions may help relieve anxieties or postregistration blues:

- Confirm with operational managers that jobs are available for team members.

- Close out the registration team with one-on-one debriefing.

- Thank team participants.

- Thank organizational participants.

- Make the transition to the maintenance team.

- Provide training for the maintenance team.

- Be aware of fatigue, burn-out, paperwork problems, and other registrar issues.

- Keep individuals aware of future or pending job opportunities.

- Enlist the help of human resource advisors.

REVIEW THE PROJECT

At the end of the registration project, you may have to evaluate the team members and suggest remuneration. Did the team members report to you directly or to functional management? If they reported to you, it's a relatively straightforward appraisal.

How should the review be conducted? Your organization may have several standard methods for reviewing employee and team performance. These are probably satisfactory, but consider the following other methods:

- *Management by objectives*   Did the person or team meet the objectives?

- *Essay*   This written approach focuses on successful accomplishments and suggestions for improvement.

- *Team approach*   How well did the individual work as part of the team?

- *Corrective action*   How well did the person deal with and correct unexpected problems?

- *Problem solving*   How well did the person solve problems individually and as part of the team?

- *Stakeholder review*   How well did the person and the team satisfy stakeholder requirements, including internal customers?

If the team members report to a functional or business unit manager, then the team leader can

- Write a report of the individual's contributions,

- Prepare an oral report about the individual's contributions,

- Defer to the functional manager, who will do the evaluation,

- Have organizational stakeholders evaluate the team members and the leader, or

- Have top management evaluate the ISO 9000 project.

RECOGNITION

Who should get the credit for ISO 9000 registration? During the project, the ISO 9000 registration leader and the team members were the people facilitating, planning, organizing, and perhaps executing the project. However, focusing only on the team can be a disservice to the organization. The organization—including top management, line management, and line employees—should receive the final kudos. The ISO 9000 team levered itself through line management to obtain registration. Staff and line teams may have written the procedures and will maintain the quality systems once registration is achieved. Although attention may have been focused on the team during the registration process, it should be refocused on the organization once registration has been achieved.

Saying thanks and acknowledging accomplishments are important throughout registration. ISO 9000 team members get recognition through team involvement, presentations, newsletters, and other means. What about the many people who also contributed but are not on the ISO 9000 team? Other employees took over the responsibilities of the team members. Employees wrote procedures and work instructions. Perhaps processes were changed and systems and processes were stabilized. People worked overtime. Operational managers put in extra work. These people also need to receive recognition.

Should the team be given monetary rewards? Some maintain that ISO 9000 registration is simply good management and that implementation should be its own reward. It improves the quality of work life and empowers employees. Others maintain that it is a special project and that special inducements—such as privileges, monies, recognition, titles, promotions, or other nonmonetary rewards—should be awarded to members. Others say nonmonetary awards are sufficient. The answer to this question varies depending on the industry, history of such projects, success of the ISO 9000 registration, organizational culture, personalities, and so forth.

THE MOST CRITICAL QUESTION: DO I STILL HAVE A JOB?

Do the ISO 9000 team members still have jobs to return to? During the registration process, have they been "out of sight and out of mind" for too long? Once ISO 9000 registration is secured, line management may determine that a particular position is not essential to operations. It may assign a particular job to others. An employee may be assigned to a pool or temporary assignment. All too often, ISO 9000 coordinators find themselves removed from the payroll. Preferably, the team members and their leaders should know what their next assignment is following registration.

Once registration has been achieved then it must be maintained. Depending on your registrar, you will be surveillance-audited yearly or every six months.

MAINTAIN QUALITY SYSTEMS

Maintaining ISO 9000 registration is just as important as achieving registration. The critical management function in this stage of the ISO 9000 process is control. Procedures have been written about how work is conducted. Systems have been established, are in control, are effective, and should continue to improve. Internal audits are periodically conducted so that if there is a problem, corrective action eliminates both the symptom and the root cause.

FIVE CONTROL FUNCTIONS

The ISO 9000 registration team may have developed the quality systems and written procedures, but line operations are now responsible for maintaining them. Five control functions are critical to maintaining quality systems and maintaining the ISO 9000 registration:

- *Monitoring*   Processes and systems are monitored continuously through sampling, statistical process control, or inspection. Procedures are current and complete.

- *Measuring*   Monitoring involves some type of measurement. Critical process or product variables are measured using calibrated instruments.

- *Evaluating*   Measured data is evaluated against the specification target and the range of the specification.

- *Correcting*   Deficiencies occur if measured data is out of specification or out of control. These deficiencies are corrected as they occur, and the process is continuously monitored to ensure that the deficiencies don't recur.

- *Preventing* The goals are to prevent deficiencies from occurring or recurring and to continuously improve processes.

ESTABLISHING A MAINTENANCE TEAM

The ISO 9000 registration team is a project team whose express goal is successful ISO 9000 registration, but day-to-day maintenance of the quality systems is an operational responsibility. There is no reason to develop a permanent ISO 9000 administrative bureaucracy. Overall maintenance involves organizational overview and documentation overview. ISO 9001 specifically states that a company shall appoint a management representative to ensure that specific ISO 9000 quality system requirements are implemented and maintained. Maintenance includes reviewing quality documents, preparing for surveillance visits, communicating with the registrar, training new personnel on quality systems, and conducting internal audits.

In a small organization, maintenance of the registration can be part of one person's quality job. In a larger organization, a management representative may be assigned to chair an informal maintenance team to deal with multidisciplinary or multiplant ISO 9000 problems. The team would meet whenever a surveillance audit is conducted, an internal audit is conducted, or a customer deficiency finding needs to be addressed. As with the registration team, the maintenance team would consist of various experts who can respond to operational problems, especially those affecting multiple processes, different suppliers, or even multiple business units.

Another option following registration is to assign members of the registration team to the maintenance effort. ISO 9000 team members already

- Know ISO 9000-related problems and solutions,

- Have developed ISO 9000 documentation,

- Have established organizational trust and rapport,

- Know ISO 9000 requirements and how to satisfy the registrar,

- Are familiar with the registration steps,

- Are a problem-solving resource, and

- Can conduct operational training and auditing.

SURVEILLANCE AUDITS

THE TYPICAL SURVEILLANCE AUDIT

Surveillance audits are biyearly or yearly periodic quality audits conducted by your registrar. The frequency with which they're conducted depends on the registrar. Their purpose is to ensure that quality systems are operating properly and that documentation is complete and current. The typical surveillance audit follows this pattern. Let's assume that a ISO 9001 compliance audit is conducted every six months and that a full recertification audit is conducted every three years. ISO 9001 incorporates all twenty quality systems. In order to evaluate all twenty systems over the three-year period, the audit team will evaluate three to four different quality systems during each surveillance audit. During the three-year cycle, each quality system is evaluated at least once.

Some auditors will check two particular quality systems on each audit—the internal quality audit and corrective action quality systems. Why? These quality systems ensure that the registrant is maintaining, controlling, and perhaps improving its quality. An internal quality audit ensures that the company is conducting periodic internal assessments. If there are deficiencies, the corrective action quality system ensures that these deficiencies are investigated, corrected, and eliminated so they don't recur. The goal is to continuously monitor the internal quality systems and improve them by minimizing variation over time.

At a small site of less than 200 people, one auditor will take two days to assess the quality systems and check compliance. With larger sites or multiple facilities, the auditor or team may take longer. Other factors that may extend the audit include verifying special tests or investigating critical discrepancies. The team may also assess the effectiveness of the corrective action of the last audit. If discrepancies were noted, the team will ensure that the problem didn't recur.

The surveillance audit may be a cursory or extensive examination. It comes down to risk and assurance again. If the registrant has had a history of multiple corrective actions and its quality systems are difficult to control, the audit is more extensive and intensive.

AN ALTERNATE MODEL OF SURVEILLANCE AUDIT

Some registrars follow a different process. When the registrar issues a registration certificate, there is no expiration date. Instead, the registrar views the postregistration process as a continuous assessment. With this model, the registrar does not use the term *surveillance assessment*. The registration certificate is valid as long as the registrant maintains its quality systems and is in compliance with the appropriate ISO 9000 standard.

The continuous assessment process begins when the registration certificate is issued. Based on the complexity of the registrant's products, effectiveness of its quality systems, and evaluation of the risks, the lead auditor after the initial audit will recommend the frequency and duration of announced or even unannounced subsequent audits. For example, if the company has a history of recurring and chronic deficiencies that can't be root cause corrected, then the lead auditor will recommend frequent and continuous assessment.[1]

FREQUENCY OF SURVEILLANCE AUDITS

Registrars conduct periodic surveillance audits to ensure that the registration maintains compliance with the appropriate ISO 9000 standard. The periodic surveillance can occur every six months, every year, or never. Why is there this variation in audit frequency? There is no international consensus concerning the frequency for surveillance audits and recertification audits. Registrars often follow different practices for conducting audits, which causes more confusion. To create more registration and auditing consistency, U.S. accredited registrars have formed a coalition called the Independent Association of Accredited Registrars. Surveillance audits among U.S. registrars are conducted once every six months or once a year.

The frequency and extensiveness of surveillance audits are determined by the level of risk and assurance required by the registrar. In general, the higher the risk of noncompliance, quality systems failure, chronic deficiencies, or product recall, the higher the level of required assurance.

RECERTIFICATION AUDITS

Recertification is usually conducted every three years. Again, there is some variation in this requirement. Some registrars, more often registrars outside the United States, don't require full recertification. They feel that periodic surveillance audits provide enough assurance to them, to customers, and to potential certification users of ISO 9000 compliance. The marketplace has largely dictated how often recertification audits are conducted. In the United States to be uniform, most registrars have opted for three-year full recertification audits. U.S. accreditors and registrars see recertification audits as a necessary requirement of ongoing and improving quality and not simply of ISO 9000 compliance.

IMPORTANCE OF JOINT PLANNING

Are audits announced or unannounced? Again, usually this condition is negotiated with the registrars. Most U.S. registrars conduct announced and jointly planned audits. The registrar will inform you when the audit will be conducted, what is required, and what quality systems will be evaluated.

Surveillance audits are planned up to six months before they are conducted. Joint planning benefits both the registrar and the registrant. The registrar wants to have auditors available to conduct the audit. The registrant wants to know when the registrar is going to visit so that it can ensure that operations are not disrupted, people are available for interviewing, facilities and tests are available for examination, and documentation is current, complete, and in compliance.

USEFULNESS OF SURVEILLANCE AUDITS

Some registered companies view surveillance audits as another mechanism by which consultants generate revenue. These companies say that surveillance audits add cost and not value and that surveillance audits are redundant. They maintain that audits are another examination of quality systems that are already in control, capable, and improving.

ISO 9000 registration is mainly the result of a customer-supplier agreement. The customer wants assurance that quality systems are in place and operating successfully. If there is another means to satisfy the customer, then it should be used. The registrant also has the opportunity to shop for registrars that don't require periodic surveillance audits.

Registration Suspension

Sometimes a registrar will suspend or cancel a registration certificate. Suspension or cancellation is not done lightly and follows only a flagrant or continuing violation. The following is a list of conditions or circumstances that will lead a registrar to suspend a certificate:

- The registrant has not informed the registrar of major changes in the certified quality systems.

- Fraud, negligence, or other actions by the registrant may impugn the registrar's reputation.

- The registrar's marks are used improperly.

- The registrar's requested corrective action requests have not been implemented.

Sometimes, registrations are canceled. The following are circumstances where this has or may happen:

- The registrant does not correct major symptoms and root cause deficiencies.

- The registrant does not pay the registrar.

- Suspension has not been cleared up after several requests.

- The registrant acts in a fraudulent or highly negligent manner.

In general, being audited periodically

- Provides your customers with assurance of quality system maintenance,

- Provides an outside perspective of your quality systems,

- Focuses on improvement of operations, and

- Communicates an internal commitment to ISO 9000 registration.

CRAMMING AND OTHER MISCONCEPTIONS

Registration is continuous as long as there is ISO 9000 compliance, assuming quality systems controls are in place, operating properly, and documented properly. If the registrant maintains and improves its quality systems and processes, then the registrar will have to conduct only a cursory check.

Cramming for the surveillance audit is difficult. The registrant should conduct internal audits periodically in critical areas after the last surveillance or full audit. Professional auditors will discover inadequacies, discrepancies, or total noncompliance through evaluating internal control and corrective action quality systems. The auditor will verify that problems didn't recur. The auditor may check the calibration dates on measuring equipment, approvals of quality procedures, and the completeness of the design and contract reviews. Were corrective actions from the last surveillance audit implemented? Did the deficiency or problem recur? How often are internal audits conducted?

CONTINUOUS IMPROVEMENT

The status quo and comfort levels are being challenged in all organizations. Creative chaos, not inertia, is now the prevalent driver of organizations. Status quo implies comfort and defense of the way things are done. In a fast-moving market, complacency can create mediocrity.

On the other hand, a proactive attitude toward quality systems prevention and improvement leads to a more competitive posture. The way work is done is changing. This can be seen in how engineers and salespeople do their respective tasks. Engineers traditionally designed and developed products in a vacuum. Salespeople sold products through established relationships. Engineers now actively solicit input from salespeople and operate as part of teams to assist in developing customer satisfying products. Sales professionals solicit engineering input to improve their sales presentation, broaden their knowledge of the products they sell and service, improve their after-sales service, and offer management new ideas. In much the same way, quality systems are used to integrate processes, eliminate non-value-adding process steps, and improve continuously.

For ISO 9000 quality systems implementation to be successful, ISO 9000 proceduralization must become part of the daily work routine. The ISO 9000 procedures and work instructions form the baseline from which new improvements occur. The internal audit becomes the process for encouraging and reviewing system improvements, which become self-sustaining. Employees—through quality of work life, suggestion systems, or through other means—lead to continuing improvement.

Quality system maintenance and improvement should evolve to become part of the day-to-day business. Critical processes and systems are stabilized and improved. They are in statistical control, and variation is continuously minimized.

APPENDIX

1. **Partial list of U.S. and Canadian Registrars**
2. **Sample Quality Manual—Level I Documentation**
3. **Examples of ISO 9000 Quality Procedures— Level II Documentation**
4. **Examples of ISO 9000 Work Instructions— Level III Documentation**
5. **Examples of Quality ISO 9000 Forms— Level IV Documentation**

PARTIAL LIST OF U.S. AND CANADIAN REGISTRARS

The list of registrars continues to grow. Many are accredited, others are pursuing accreditation, and others are going their own way. Regardless of their status, evaluate each registrar closely in terms of satisfying your needs. One caveat: no attempt has been made to assess these registrars. Carefully evaluate each one to find the right one for you.

ABS Quality Evaluations
16855 Northchase Drive
Houston, TX 77060
Phone (713) 873-9400
FAX (713) 874-9564

American Association for Laboratory
  Accreditation (A2LA)
656 Quince Orchard Road, #704
Gaithersburg, MD 20878
Phone (301) 670-1377
FAX (301) 869-1495

American Certification Corp.
3582 Whispering Brook Court
Grand Rapids, MI 49508
Phone (616) 452-8374
FAX (616) 452-8374

American European Services
1054 31st Street, NW, Suite 120
Washington, DC 20007
Phone (202) 337-3214
FAX (202) 377-3709

American Quality Assessors
1201 Main Street, Suite 2010
P.O. Box 1149
Columbia, SC 29201
Phone (803) 254-1164
FAX (803) 252-0056

A.G.A. Quality/International Approval
  Services
8501 East Pleasant Valley Road
Cleveland, OH 44131
Phone (216) 524-4990
FAX (216) 642-3463

American Society for Mechanical
  Engineers
345 East 47th Street, 39W
New York, NY 10017
Phone (212) 605-4796
FAX (212) 605-8713

American Software Quality Assurance
3187 Blue Rock Road
Cincinnati, OH 45239
Phone (800) 822-4289
FAX (800) 822-4289

AT&T Quality Registrars
2600 San Tomas Expressway
Santa Clara, CA 95051
Phone (800) 521-3399
FAX (408) 522-4436

AV Quality
2900 Wilcrest, Suite 300
Houston, TX 77042
Phone (713) 465-2850
FAX (713) 465-1182

Bellcore Quality Registration
6 Corporate Place
Piscataway, NJ 08854
Phone (908) 699-3739
FAX (908) 336-2244

British Standards Institution
8000 Towers Crescent Drive, Suite 1350
Vienna, VA 22182
Phone (703) 760-7828
FAX (703) 760-8999

Bureau Veritas Quality International
509 North Main Street
Jamestown, NY 14701
Phone (800) 937-9311
FAX (716) 484-9003

CGA Approvals
55 Scarsdale Road
Don Mills, Ontario M3B 2R3
Canada
Phone (416) 447-6465
FAX (416) 447-7076

Canadian General Standards Board
Conformity Assessment Branch
222 Queen Street, Suite 1402
Ottawa, Ontario K1A 1G6
Canada
Phone (613) 941-8709
FAX (613) 941-8706

Davy Registrar Services
One Oliver Plaza
Pittsburgh, PA 15222
Phone (412) 566-4500
FAX (412) 566-3229

Det Norske Veritas Industry, Inc.
16340 Park Ten Place, Suite 100
Houston, TX 77084
Phone (713) 579-9003
FAX (713) 579-1360

DLS Quality Technology Associates, Inc.
108 Hallmore Drive
Camillus, NY 13031
Phone (315) 468-5811
FAX (315) 637-2707

Electronics Industries Association
    Quality Registry
2001 Pennsylvania Avenue, NW
Washington, DC 20006
Phone (202) 457-4970
FAX (202) 457-4985

Entela, Inc.
3033 Madison, SW
Grand Rapids, MI 49548
Phone (616) 247-0515
FAX (616) 247-7527

ETL Testing Laboratories
Industrial Park
Cortland, NY 13045
Phone (607) 753-6711
FAX (607) 756-9891

Factory Mutual Research Corp.
1151 Boston-Providence Turnpike
P.O. Box 9102
Norwood, MA 02062
Phone (617) 255-4883
FAX (617) 762-9375

Groupement Quebeçois de Certification
de la Qualité
220-70 rue Dalhousie
Quebec City, Quebec G1K 4B2
Canada
Phone (418) 643-5813
FAX (418) 646-3315

Intertek Services Corp
9900 Main Street, Suite 500
Fairfax, VA 22031
Phone (703) ISO-9000
FAX (703) 273-2895

KEMA Registered Quality
4379 County Line Road
Chalfont, PA 18914
Phone (215) 822-4281
FAX (215) 822-4271

KPMG Peat Marwick
Three Chestnut Ridge Road
Montvale, NJ 07645
Phone (201) 307-7900
FAX (201) 307-7991

Litton Systems Canada, Ltd.
25 City View Drive
Etobicoke, Ontario M9W 5A7
Phone (416) 249-1231
FAX (416) 245-0324

Lloyd's Register Quality Assurance
33–41 Newark Street
Hoboken, NJ 07030
Phone (201) 693-1111
FAX (201) 963-3299

MET Electrical Testing Co.
916 Patapsco Avenue
Baltimore, MD 21230
Phone (410) 354-2200
FAX (410) 354-1624

Moody International Quality Assurance
Register, Inc.
350 McKnight Plaza Building
105 Braunlich Drive
Pittsburgh, PA 15237
Phone (412) 366-5567
FAX (412) 366-5571

National Quality Assurance
1146 Massachusetts Avenue
Boxborough, MA 01719
Phone (508) 635-9256
FAX (508) 266-1073

NSF International
3475 Plymouth Road
P.O. Box 130140
Ann Arbor, MI 48113
Phone (313) 769-8010
FAX (313) 769-0109

National Standards Authority of Ireland
5 Medallion Centre
Greenly Street
Merrimack, NH 03054
Phone (603) 424-7070
FAX (603) 429-1427

OTS Quality Registrars
10700 Northwest Freeway, Suite 455
Houston, TX 77092
Phone (713) 688-9494
FAX (713) 688-9590

Quality Management Institute
Mississauga Executive Centre, Suite 800
2 Robert Speck Parkway
Mississauga, Ontario, L4Z 1H8
Canada
Phone (416) 272-3920
FAX (416) 272-3942

Quality Systems Registrars, Inc.
13873 Park Center Road, Suite 217
Herndon, VA 22071
Phone (703) 478-0241
FAX (703) 478-0645

Scott Quality Systems Registrars, Inc.
40 Washington Street
Wellesley Hills, MA 02181
Phone (617) 239-1110
FAX (617) 239-0433

SGS International Certification Services,
  Inc.
1415 Park Avenue
Hoboken, NJ 07030
Phone (201) 792-2400
FAX (201) 792-2558

Smithers Quality Assurance, Inc.
425 West Market Street
Akron, OH 44303
Phone (216) 762-4231
FAX (216) 762-7447

Southwest Research Institute
P.O. Drawer 28510
6220 Culbra Road
San Antonio, TX 78288
Phone (210) 522-2942
FAX (210) 522-3692

Steel Related Industries Quality System
  Registrar
2000 Corporate Drive, Suite 450
Wexford, PA 15090
Phone (412) 935-2844
FAX (412) 935-6825

Testwell Craig Laboratories, Inc.
47 Hudson Street
Ossining, NY 10562
Phone: (914) 762-9000
FAX (914) 762-9638

TRA Certification
700 East Beardsley Avenue
P.O. Box 1081
Elkhart, IN 46515
Phone (219) 264-0745
FAX (210) 264-0740

Tri-Tech Services
4700 Clairton Boulevard
Pittsburgh, PA 15236
Phone (412) 884-2290
FAX (412) 884-2268

TUV America
5 Cherry Hill Drive
Danvers, MA 01923
Phone (508) 777-7999
FAX (508) 777-8441

RTI/TUV Essen
1032 Elwell Court, Suite 222
Palo Alto, CA 94303
Phone (415) 961-0521
FAX (415) 961-9119

TUV Rheinland of North America, Inc.
12 Commerce Road
Newton, CT 06470
Phone (203) 426-0888
FAX (203) 270-8883

Underwriter's Laboratories, Inc.
Quality and Reliability Department
1285 Walt Whitman Rd.
Melville, NY 11747
Phone (516) 271-6200
FAX (516) 271-8259

Underwriter's Laboratories of Canada
Quality Registry Division
7 Crouse Road
Scarborough, Ontario M1R 3A9
Canada
Phone (416) 757-3611
FAX (416) 757-9540

Warnock Hersey Professional Services
  Limited
128 Elmslie Street
LaSalle, Quebec H8R 1V8
Canada
Phone (514) 366-3100
FAX (514) 366-5350

SAMPLE QUALITY MANUAL

ISO 9001: 4.1
MANAGEMENT RESPONSIBILITY

1.0 **Quality Policy.** QM anticipates and exceeds customer's requirements and expectations through cost-competitive quality products and service that are delivered on time, every time.

1.1 QM's executive management is totally committed to total customer satisfaction through cost-competitive quality products and services. Senior management presents quarterly updates of new companywide quality policies and procedures.

2.0 **Organization.** QM's quality organization personnel have the authority and responsibility to maintain, implement, and update QM's quality system. This includes
  • Defining customer quality requirements,
  • Specifying system, process, and product quality requirements,
  • Initiating corrective action to prevent nonconformances,
  • Identifying and recording nonconformances through organizational channels,
  • Initiating changes to eliminate symptoms and root causes, and
  • Verifying effectiveness of corrective action.

2.1 All QM personnel are responsible for verifying system and product compliance to QM policies and procedures. Quality systems auditing is conducted in all company operations by trained, independent, and objective individuals.

2.2 QM has a corporate representative responsible for maintaining and ensuring ISO 9001 quality system registration; for conducting corporate internal quality audits; for ensuring improvement of internal quality systems; and for liaisoning with external parties concerning the organization's quality systems. The corporate representative is Jane Smith. The business unit person is the quality vice president. The plant person is the quality assurance manager.

3.0 **Management Review of Quality Systems** QM's quality policies, procedures, and overall quality system are periodically reviewed by management and audited by business unit and plant-designated personnel.

3.1 The overall total quality management system is audited and reviewed at the corporate, business unit, and plant levels at least once a year. The head of quality at each organizational level is responsible for the audit. The review covers

- Complete, current, and accurate specifications,
- Application of procedures,
- Quality manual completeness, and
- Corrective action effectiveness.

Management reviews quality strategic plans, tactical plans, accountabilities, policies, procedures and benchmarks to improve operational effectiveness, efficiency, and economy. Records of all reviews and audits are maintained at the QM corporate quality office.

ISO 9001: 4.2
QUALITY SYSTEM

1.0 **General Quality System** QM maintains an organization, the personnel, and the quality systems to ensure external and internal customer satisfaction through cost-competitive quality products and services.

1.1 QM maintains total quality management systems to ensure internal and external customer satisfaction in its products and services.

1.2 ISO 9001 forms the foundation and structure of all QM6s quality systems. QM's corporate and business unit quality manuals define current policies and procedure for complying with the latest ISO 9001 revision. Each site has its own specific quality documentation, including policies and work instructions detailing the control and management of quality.

1.3 QM's quality systems are certified and registered by quality science registrars. QM notifies the registrar of significant quality system changes. The quality officer of the appropriate organizational level is responsible for notifying the registrar.

2.0 **Quality Systems Documentation** Quality systems documentation includes quality policies, procedures, work instructions, and other documentation. ISO 9001 quality policies and procedures are incorporated into the corporate and business unit quality manuals.

2.1 Quality manual numbering corresponds to ISO 9001 clauses.

3.0 **Quality Plan** QM has developed quality plans to ensure operational consistency and prevent nonconformances. Quality analysis planning involves all operational personnel, including professional, administrative, service, and production. The goal of quality planning is to ensure customer satisfaction through the delivery of quality products and services. Quality plans are developed for each new contract, new product, modified product, or process change. Quality plans will include but are not limited by the following:

- Control and improvement of quality through the acquisition of new products, processes, equipment, people, or other resources.
- Identify and define quality process and product characteristics.
- Ensure the compatibility of design, manufacturing, purchasing, test, and delivery procedures and documentation.
- Update quality control processes and procedures to maintain and improve quality.
- Identify measurement or process capability requirements that surpass equipment ability.
- Identify quality controls throughout product development, purchasing, manufacturing, and delivery cycles.
- Maintain and update required quality documentation.

4.0 **Quality Records**. Quality documentation is maintained according to quality procedures.

5.0 **Responsibility** The chief quality officer of the operational unit is responsible for ensuring that quality procedures are monitored and improved. All employees are responsible for following quality procedures and for continuous, measurable improvement.

5.1 QM quality management reviews quality policies, systems, procedures, and documentation. Quality audits and reviews focus on efficiency, effectiveness, and economy.

ISO 9001: 4.3
CONTRACT REVIEW

1.0 **Contract Requirements** Customer documentation and contracts are reviewed prior to acceptance to ensure that customer requirements are defined and understood. This applies to all types of contract orders, including written, verbal, or other types. QM quality organization identifies internal parties who should review new contracts. Before acceptance, all internal parties will review and approve new contract requirements. The following contractual quality documentation are periodically reviewed:

- Purchase orders,
- Product and process specifications,
- Quality plans,
- Control and capability requirements, and
- Special instructions or requirements.

2.0 Customer Contract Review New or modified product contracts are reviewed to ensure that

- New requirements are defined and understood,
- New requirements can be complied with, and
- New requirements are properly reviewed by all parties.

3.0 New product development Customer satisfaction, defect prevention, and continuous improvement are key elements of new product development.

4.0 Capabilities Existing and new product contracts are evaluated in terms of QM's ability to satisfy customer requirements. Equipment, environment personnel, engineering, manufacturing, methods, tooling, and other systems are evaluated.

5.0 Records Contract review records are maintained and accessible to all QM parties. External party review must be approved by QM management.

ISO 9001: 4.4
DESIGN CONTROL

1.0 Design Development and Planning Designs are controlled and planned throughout product development to ensure that specified requirements are satisfied. Design output and input variables are identified, controlled, monitored, measured, and documented throughout product development.

1.1 Product design and verification activities are planned by and assigned to quality representatives for review. Critical individuals for reviewing designs are identified. Design changes are documented and reviewed by designated individuals.

1.2 Design control information is documented, communicated, and reviewed throughout product development.

2.0 Design Input Product requirements are identified and documented. Groups with specific expertise that can contribute are identified. Regulatory, safety, and health requirements are identified and reviewed for adequacy and compliance. Conflicting requirements are resolved by QM project and product managers.

3.0 Design Output Design output is documented in terms of satisfying customer requirements by

- Meeting design input requirements,
- Defining process and product requirements,
- Containing acceptance criteria,

- Conforming to industry requirements and government regulations, and
- Classifying and prioritizing product attributes that deal with safety, health, consumer protection, or environmental conditions.

4.0 Design Verification Designs are planned, documented, and verified throughout the product-development process. Design verification involves the following:

- Holding design reviews,
- Conducting reliability testing,
- Analyzing design calculations,
- Comparing designs against competitors' products,
- Conducting independent analysis,
- Testing products in different environments,
- Reviewing all design-related documents, and
- Reviewing safety and health issues.

5.0 Design Changes Design modifications, changes, or revisions are monitored, controlled, verified, validated, and documented through the engineering change order (ECO) system. The ECO system is close-looped so that it identifies changes, permits reviews of the changes, and secures approvals. Authorized personnel sign off on all design changes.

ISO 9001: 4.5
DOCUMENT AND DATA CONTROL

1.0 Approval and Issue Quality systems are documented and controlled. Control involves the issue, approval, review, distribution, and modification of documents.

1.1 ISO 9000 and customer documents are available at appropriate operational locations involving quality systems. If necessary, customer, regulatory, and other critical documents are available at the business unit's or corporate quality office.

2.0 Changes and Modifications Documentation change and modifications are approved by authorized personnel before issuance. A master list of approved changes to quality documentation is maintained and controlled by the site quality personnel. Control includes the following:

- Quality documentation is readily available by site personnel.
- Obsolete documents are removed from manuals, computers, and other locations.
- Obsolete regulatory-, health-, or safety-related documents are maintained if required by QM's legal department.

Document and data changes are reviewed and approved by the same functional groups and preferably by the same personnel that initially approved the documentation.

ISO 9001: 4.6
PURCHASING

1.0 **Selection of Suppliers** Suppliers of products and services are selected, monitored, and improved through specified requirements involving quality, delivery, service, and cost.

1.1 Suppliers are selected based on the following criteria:
- Past history,
- Process control site audit,
- Process control and capability,
- Self-assessment,
- Product inspection and testing,
- Performance history, and
- Reliability, maintainability, and other testing.

1.2 Each business unit maintains and evaluates records of supplier performance.

2.0 **Purchasing Data and Documentation** Purchasing information is documented, current, complete, and accurate.

2.1 All purchasing and customer documentation is retained, including
- Purchase order,
- Engineering prints,
- Supplier evaluation forms, and
- Product test data.

2.2 QM quality representatives review and approve all customer and supplier documentation throughout product development and product life cycles.

2.3 Customer requirements and expectations are fully described in documentation, including
- Type, number, level, and other data of required materials,
- Type of services,
- Acceptance levels,
- Delivery requirements,
- Costs,
- Performance requirements,
- Engineering and manufacturing process, and
- Corrective actions.

2.4 QM retains the right to audit on-site supplier processes, testing, or other supplier activities. The supplier is still responsible for satisfying contract requirements and for proving acceptable products.

ISO 9001: 4.7
CONTROL OF CUSTOMER SUPPLIED PRODUCT

1.0 **Procedures** Procedures are established for specifying, identifying, handling, transporting, and storing purchased materials.

1.1 Qualified stores' personnel identify, count, and verify that supplied materials conform to contract and quality requirements. Conforming and nonconforming materials are segregated, stored, handled, and tagged according to procedures.

1.2 Purchased materials are stored, handled, and transported according to approved procedures and industry standards.

2.0 **Lost, Damaged, or Unsuitable Materials** Lost, damaged, or unsuitable materials are documented and reported to the customer.

3.0 **Responsibility** Responsibility for meeting QM's requirements still rests with the supplier.

ISO 9001: 4.8
PRODUCT IDENTIFICATION AND TRACEABILITY

1.0 **Material and Product Identification** Procedures are established and maintained to identify and document materials and products throughout product development and the product life cycles.

2.0 **Traceability** In-house and purchased materials are traced through product development and the product life cycles. Traceability also extends to delivery and installation. If required by contract, QM can identify individual batches, shipments, or products.

ISO 9001: 4.9
PROCESS CONTROL

1.0 **General Processes** All major organizational processes are controlled. If applicable, processes are in control and capable.

1.1 Process control may include documented procedures, trained employees, statistically controlled machinery, process approval, workmanship criteria, monitored environments, and calibrated equipment. Procedure and work instructions are developed for each job, and employees understand responsibilities. Quality systems are evaluated periodically to ensure that they are current, accurate, and complete. Internal customer satisfaction is also monitored.

2.0 **Special Processes** Special processes are those that are operator dependent.

2.1 Special processes are monitored and controlled.

2.2 Process control requirements are defined for all process variables.

2.3 Outputs from special process are monitored to ensure that they comply with specification, procedures, and instructions.

2.4 Records are maintained and available for special processes, equipment, and personnel.

ISO 9001: 4.10
INSPECTION AND TESTING

1.0 **Receiving Inspection and Testing** Materials and products are inspected according to documented procedures that ensure conformance to specifications. Required inspection and testing are detailed in quality plans.

1.1 Receiving inspection ensures that incoming materials conform to quality specifications. If materials cannot or are not inspected, then certifications of compliance may be required from the supplier. Materials from certified suppliers are not inspected.

1.2 The quality organization is responsible for generating and controlling inspection reports and supplier quality documentation.

1.3 First-item sample products from suppliers are evaluated by the quality and engineering organization. Results are communicated to purchasing for supplier approval. First-item samples must be received and evaluated prior to production. First-item samples are required for new products, modifications of existing products, new suppliers, or new processes. Engineering, quality, manufacturing, and purchasing must sign off on the first-item samples. On acceptance, an approval document is generated with test results. Purchasing is responsible for communicating approval to the supplier. If the sample is rejected, all documentation is sent to purchasing, which communicates the reasons and alternative to the supplier.

1.4 If material is urgently required, engineering, quality, manufacturing, and purchasing jointly approve the waiver.

2.0 **In-process Inspection and Testing** In-process testing and inspection stations are identified on a flow chart, quality plan, or similar document. Supplementary documentation identifies type of inspection, product characteristics, inspection methods, inspection methods, inspection levels, AQLs, (Acceptable Quality Levels) and inspection equipment.

3.0 **Final Inspection and Testing** Final testing and inspection stations are identified on a flow chart, quality plan, or similar document. Supplementary documentation identifies type of inspection, product characteristics, inspection methods, inspection levels, AQLs, and inspection equipment.

4.0 **Inspection and Test Records** Inspection and test records are maintained and indicate conformance. The quality plan details all specified inspection and tests, locations, results, and disposition of products.

ISO 9001: 4.11
CONTROL OF INSPECTION, MEASURING, AND TEST EQUIPMENT

1.0 **General Requirements** During product development, key product characteristics are identified on engineering prints or similar documents. Inspection, measuring, and test equipment are identified to measure the previously indicated product characteristic accurately and precisely. Inspection, measurement, and test equipment are calibrated for precision and accuracy. Calibration status is recorded on gages and on quality documentation. Test software is also controlled to determine ability to determine product conformance. In-house reference calibration is conducted in controlled conditions. Inspection, measurement, and test are all proceduralized. Internal reference gages and external calibration service are transferable to NIST (National Institute for Standards and Technology).

2.0 **Responsibilities** Responsibilities for inspection, measurement, and testing are detailed. Organization personnel are responsible for checking and ensuring accurate and precise measurement equipment. Measurement equipment is stored, handled, and secured according to procedures.

3.0 **Specific Requirements** The following are specific requests for measurement equipment:

- Product and process measurements are identified.
- Measuring equipment is properly identified.
- Location, calibration date, calibration frequency, authority, and other criteria are documented.
- Damaged or uncalibrated equipment is segregated.
- Calibration processes are evaluated.
- Calibration records are maintained.
- Previous calibration accuracy is validated if necessary.
- Environmental conditions are checked.
- Handling, storage, and security of measuring equipment is checked.

ISO 9001: 4.12
INSPECTION AND TEST STATUS

1.0 **Identification** Inspection and test status of product are identified throughout production. Nonconforming products are properly tagged and segregated. Conforming products are released to the next production step only if identification indicates proper release status. Identification must follow procedures and may include tags, labels, or marks.

2.0 **Authority** Release authority for conforming products are identified on products, lots, or shipments.

ISO 9001: 4.13
CONTROL OF NONCONFORMING PRODUCT

1.0 **Control of Nonconforming Material and Products** Nonconforming products are identified, evaluated, segregated, and disposed of according to procedures. Quality procedures detail responsibility and authority for determining the cause and disposing of nonconforming material and products.

2.0 **Review and Inspection** Nonconforming materials are reviewed according to procedures. They may be
- Scrapped,
- Reworked,
- Used as is,
- Returned to the supplier, or
- Regraded.

3.0 Nonconforming products are retained or disposed of according to procedures. Repaired or reworked products are reinspected according to inspection procedures. Records are maintained of any action dealing with materials.

ISO 9001: 4.14
CORRECTIVE AND PREVENTIVE ACTION

1.0 **General Purpose** Corrective and preventive action are planned and documented. Corrective action focuses on eliminating the symptom and the root cause. Preventive action focuses on eliminating occurrences and recurrences.

2.0 **Corrective Action** Nonconformances, flaws, or deficiencies are prioritized, and the most significant are analyzed and eliminated first. Some of the analysis tools used are cost of quality, statistical process control (SPC), customer complaints, and inspection results. Corrective action also involves
- Analyzing customer complaints,
- Analyzing product nonconformances,
- Investigating the cause of the above nonconformances,
- Determining the cause of corrective actions, and
- Applying controls to prevent recurrence.

3.0 **Preventive Action** The goal of preventive action is to prevent occurrences and recurrences. The results of preventive action are investigated to ensure that problems do not recur. Preventive action also involves
- Analyzing data and information to detect and analyze potential causes of nonconformances,
- Developing a plan to prevent occurrences and recurrences or nonconformances,

- Initiating preventive action, and
- Evaluating the effectiveness of preventive action.

4.0 Documentation and Records Corrective action from initiation to result is documented properly.

ISO 9001: 4.15
HANDLING, STORAGE, PACKAGING, PRESERVATION, AND DELIVERY

1.0 General Procedures Production materials are identified so there is an audit trail from incoming material to customer deliver or to final disposition. Procedures are developed for handling, storing, packaging, and delivering materials.

2.0 Handling Handling procedures ensure that materials are not damaged through the production cycle. Procedures and drawings prescribe proper containers. Procedures also detail special handling requirements.

3.0 Storage Storage procedures ensure that materials are not damaged through the production cycle. Storage procedures specially instruct personnel on maintaining proper environmental conditions.

4.0 Packaging Packaging procedures ensure that materials are not damaged throughout the production cycle. Packaging is designed to meet customer requirements, type of transportation, product, cost, and other factors.

5.0 Delivery Delivery procedure ensure that materials are not damaged during internal or external transit. Packaging accounts for misuse or abuse so materials still conform to requirements.

ISO 9001: 4.16
CONTROL OF QUALITY RECORDS

1.0 General Requirements Quality records are generated and maintained throughout the organization for all critical activities and functions, including identification, collection, indexing, access, filing, maintenance, and disposition of quality records. Quality records can be retrieved easily and are available to all personnel. Quality records are identifiable, accurate, complete, and current. Quality records are traceable and auditable to processes, products, and results.

2.0 Records Types Many types of quality records are retained, including
- Specifications,
- Quality costs,
- Supplier quality,
- Inspection and measurement,
- Internal audits,
- Design review,
- Customer complaints,

- Process quality,
- Product performance,
- Corrective action, and
- Audit results.

3.0 **Retention** Quality records are retained according to specific requirements in procedures and policies. Records are available for review by the customer. Quality records may be in electronic or hard media.

ISO 9001: 4.17
INTERNAL QUALITY AUDITS

1.0 **Audit Schedule** Quality audits are conducted to verify quality activities, quality planning compliance, and quality system effectiveness. Quality audits are prioritized based on importance, cost, and internal requirements.

2.0 **Audit Specific Requirements** Area quality organizations are responsible for planning, conducting, and reporting audit results. Quality audits are conducted by independent, trained, and qualified personnel. Audits follow documented procedures. All organizational quality processes, systems, or products are audited.

3.0 **Results** Audit reports are distributed to the specified people defined in procedures. Audited areas may be reaudited to evaluate efficiency, effectiveness, and economy of corrective action. Follow-up audits may be conducted to verify and record effectiveness of correction action.

3.1 The entire organization, business units, and plants are audited yearly to determine compliance with policies and procedures.

ISO 9001: 4.18
TRAINING

1.0 **General Requirements** All employees are trained to do their jobs properly so that the internal and ultimately the external customers are satisfied. Job requirements are spelled out to perform the required work.

2.0 **Quality Training** Quality is an essential element of the training and development of new and existing employees. Training effort are periodically evaluated and updated. Critical elements of quality training are that

- External and internal customer satisfaction is critical,
- Customers are satisfied through total quality management,
- Prevention and continuous improvement are required to keep up with changing customer expectations,
- Benchmarks are established and progress is measured, and
- Suppliers are important partners in the improvement process.

3.0 **Responsibilities** Operational and functional area heads are responsible for ensuring that training and development objectives are attained.

4.0 **Records** Training records are maintained for all employees.

5.0 **Training programs** Quality training is industry, company, process, and product specific.

ISO 9001: 4.19
SERVICING

1.0 **General Requirements** Service process, systems, and documentation properly address service requirements. After-sales service is documented so that customer requirements are satisfied. Internal and external customers are surveyed to determine customer satisfaction.

2.0 **Responsibilities** Customer service accountabilities are defined for all appropriate personnel.

3.0 **Records** Service records, including survey results, failure modes, costs, and studies are maintained and periodically assessed.

ISO 9001: 4.20
STATISTICAL TECHNIQUES

1.0 **General Requirements** Statistical techniques are established for appropriate business processes. Personnel are trained in statistical prevention. Records are maintained to record the result of statistical analysis and to pursue continuous improvement.

2.0 **Sampling Plans** Sampling and inspection plans reflect supplier's process capabilities, type of products, product characteristics, costs, and risks.

3.0 **Techniques.** The list of statistical techniques includes but is not limited to the following:

- Statistical process control (SPC),
- Taguchi methods,
- Histograms,
- Reliability calculations,
- Engineering calculations, and
- Sampling.

4.0 **Applications.** Statistical analysis is used in the following:

- Reliability testing,
- Production processes,
- Engineering product development,
- Market analysis,
- Continuous improvement, and
- Customer satisfaction.

EXAMPLES OF ISO 9000 QUALITY PROCEDURES

1. **INTERNAL QUALITY AUDITS**
2. **CORRECTIVE ACTION REQUESTS**
3. **INTRODUCTORY QUALITY TRAINING**

INTERNAL QUALITY AUDITS

1.0 **Purpose** Quality audits are periodically conducted to determine the efficiency and effectiveness of the organization's quality activities.

2.0 **Scope** This procedure applies to all internal functions and business units.

3.0 **Definitions**

Quality Audit Objective and independent appraisal of quality activities to determine compliance with customer or regulatory requirements.

Auditor Person conducting the audit.

Client Person authorizing audit.

Auditee Area being audited.

Audit plan How the audit is conducted.

Corrective Action Process of eliminating symptom and root cause of deficiency.

QSR Acronym for quality system requirements; sentence, paragraph, and number of quality system requirement.

4.0 **Procedure** The quality organization is responsible for conducting the quality audit. The internal authority—the customer—must authorize the audit. The auditee is notified of the pending audit within two weeks. The audit supervisor or manager reviews and approves the audit plan.

The quality audit follows three elements:

1. Planning,
2. Conducting, and
3. Reporting.

The auditor is responsible for developing the audit plan. The audit plan details how the audit is conducted. The plan incorporates the following:

1. Customer or client,
2. Auditor's name,
3. Auditee's area and name,
4. Program or project name,
5. ISO 9001 quality system requirement elements,
6. Audit date,
7. Audit plan or course of action, and
8. Reporting procedure.

The quality audit seeks to determine compliance with the appropriate ISO 9001 requirement. The auditor ensures that quality documents satisfy ISO 9000 requirements. First, the quality manual is reviewed for compliance. Business unit or functional area procedures and work instructions detail how work is performed.

The auditor may conduct the following tests:

- Comparing work against work instructions,
- Testing random production products to evaluate the effectiveness of test or production processes,
- Observing work methods to ensure they follow procedures,
- Analyzing deviations or deficiencies to determine their cause,
- Calculating stresses, reliability, or other quality-related problems, and
- Inspecting drawings, bills of material, or other technical documentation for accuracy, completeness, and understandability.

The auditor completes the quality assurance plan attached in these procedures. If deficiencies are discovered, then they are reported in a corrective action request. Reports are completed within one week of conducting the audit.

Quality audit reports are reviewed by the auditee and approved by the quality audit supervision. If required, follow-up audits may be conducted on request.

5.0 Relevant ISO 9001 Clauses

4.1   Management Responsibility
4.2   Quality System
4.14 Corrective and Preventive Action
4.16 Quality Records
4.17 Internal Auditing

CORRECTIVE ACTION REQUESTS

1.0 **Purpose** This procedures details a system for informing personnel of noncompliance or nonconformance to quality requirements and the need for initiating corrective actions.

2.0 **Scope** This procedure encompasses all activities, departments, internal suppliers, external suppliers, and business units of the organization. The quality department is responsible for conducting the audits and for ensuring that the report is transmitted to the appropriate parties. The auditor is not responsible for investigating the cause and determining the appropriate course of action to eliminate the symptom and the root cause.

3.0 **Definitions**

Quality Audit Objective and independent appraisal of quality activities to determine compliance with customer or regulatory requirements.

Auditor Person conducting the audit.

Client Person authorizing audit.

Auditee Area being audited.

Audit plan How the audit is conducted.

Corrective Action Process of eliminating the symptom and root cause of the deficiency.

Corrective action report Report that concludes the investigation.

4.0 **Procedure** A corrective action request (CAR) is initiated as a result of a quality systems deficiency or discrepancy. The deficiency may be discovered as a result of an audit or during the normal course of business. The goal of the CAR is to fix the symptom and to eliminate the cause.

The CAR report identifies the following:

- CAR identification number,
- Name, address, and telephone number of the auditee,
- Name, address, and telephone number of the auditor,
- Name, address, and telephone number of the customer,
- Date of request,
- Date of the audit,
- Project, product, or part number,
- Applicable regulatory or internal specifications,
- Description of the deficiency,
- Symptom and root cause,
- Conclusions, and
- Recommendations.

The quality department maintains the corrective action request status report. The report details

- CAR number,
- Recommendations,
- Name of organization responsible for correction action,
- Response effectiveness and date, and
- Recurrence of problem.

The CAR is transmitted to the customer and auditee. The auditee is responsible for determining the actual cause of the discrepancy and actions taken to prevent recurrence. The customer or auditee can request a postaudit to determine effectiveness of the corrective action.

5.0 **Relevant ISO 9001 Clauses**
4.1   Management Responsibility
4.2   Quality System
4.3   Corrective Action
4.16 Quality Records

INTRODUCTORY QUALITY TRAINING

1.0 **Purpose** This procedure details requirements for training of all company employees regarding quality product and services. All personnel will have at least 24 hours of training in quality each year.

2.0 **Scope** This procedure applies to all organizational personnel.

3.0 **Procedure** The training department and the quality assurance organization is responsible for creating and maintaining quality management, assurance, and control training requirements.

All new personnel will be trained in the organization's quality management course. All new employees also will be made familiar with the organization's quality policies and procedures. All new employees will be trained in specific quality procedures, operational methods, and work instruction. Current employees will be familiarized with new quality policies and procedures.

Quality courses are taught by immediate supervisors or quality staff personnel. Instructors have been taught and tested by approved train-the-trainer instructors.

The training department creates and maintains a list of training, education, and experience requirements for all jobs. Training requirements are reevaluated yearly. New requirements are added to the job description. Area supervision and the training department are responsible for ensuring that employees are appropriately trained.

The introductory quality course will cover
- The organization's quality vision and mission,
- Quality objectives, goals, and plans,
- ISO 9000 quality requirements,
- ISO 9000 concepts and terms,
- Internal quality audits and corrective audits,
- Employee certification, qualification, and testing,
- Quality system planning,
- Quality job instructions,
- Quality metrics, and
- Quality documentation.

New and existing employees are notified of pending sessions one month before training session. Each employee will be provided with the following:
- The purpose of the training,
- Testing requirements,
- Date of the training,
- The subject matter covered in training,
- The location of the training, and
- The instructor's name.

4.0 Relevant ISO 9001 Clauses
4.1 Management Responsibility
4.2 Quality System
4.16 Quality Records
4.18 Training

EXAMPLE OF ISO 9000 QUALITY WORK INSTRUCTIONS

CORRECTIVE ACTION REQUEST (CAR) INSTRUCTION

1. **Purpose** To communicate the result of a quality audit.

2. **Application** This instruction covers all corrective action activities throughout the company.

3. **Associated Materials**
   3.1 Corrective Action Request, Form 17.1
   3.2 Corrective Action Status Report, Form 17.2

4. **Instruction** The CAR instruction results from the results of a corrective action request, audit, field failure report, or other internal or external investigation. The CAR form, Form 17.1, is filled out as follows:

    1. CAR number,

    2. Name, location, and telephone number of the auditee,

    3. Name, location, and telephone number of the customer,

    4. Audit number and date,

    5. CAR request due date,

    6. Part number and name,

    7. Process description and location,

    8. Description of the deficiency,

    9. Description of the apparent condition,

    10. Possible or probable cause,

    11. Actual cause,

    12. Actions take to prevent recurrence, and

    13. Signature of the person responsible for correction action.

The Corrective Action Status Report, Form 17.2, is filled out as follows:

1. CAR number,

2. Audit or investigation report number,

3. Auditee name, location, and phone number responsible for corrective action,

4. Auditor name,

5. Date of CAR,

6. Response date of CAR,

7. Date of actual response, and

8. Remarks.

EXAMPLES OF QUALITY ISO 9000 FORMS

1. CORRECTIVE ACTION REQUEST FORM 17.1
2. CORRECTIVE ACTION STATUS REPORT FORM 17.2

CORRECTIVE ACTION REQUEST FORM 17.1

1. CAR number

2. Name, location, and telephone number of the auditee

3. Name, location, and telephone number of the customer

4. Audit number and date

5. CAR request due date

6. Part number and name

7. Process description and location

8. Description of the deficiency (auditor's description)

9. Description of apparent condition (auditor's description)

10. Possible or probable cause (auditor's description)

11. Actual cause (auditee's responsibility)

12. Actions taken to prevent recurrence (auditee's responsibility)

13. Signature of person responsible for correction action (auditee's responsibility)

5. CARs and status reports are maintained by the quality department. The CAR is forwarded to assigned organizations for action. The CAR is returned to the quality department, which maintains a current CAR status report.

CORRECTIVE ACTION STATUS REPORT FORM 17.2

1. CAR number

2. Audit or investigation report number

3. Auditee name, location, and phone number responsible for corrective action

4. Auditor name

5. Date of CAR

6. Response date of CAR

7. Date of actual response

8. Remarks

NOTES

Step 5 ORGANIZE FOR REGISTRATION

1. "Empowerment Boundaries at Sáturn," *Tapping the Network Journal* (Fall 1992), pp. 2–3.

Step 7 CONDUCT THE PREASSESSMENT

1. ANSI/ASQC Q91-1987. "Quality Management and Quality Assurance Standards, Guidelines for Selection Use."
2. ANSI/ASQ Q90-1987, "Quality Management and Quality Assurance Standards, Guidelines for Selection and Use," p. 2
3. ANSI/ASQC Standard Q1, "1986 Generic Guidelines for Auditing of Quality Systems."

Step 10 MAINTAIN REGISTRATION

1. G. Dzus, and E. Sykes, "How to Survive ISO 9000 Surveillance," *Quality Progress* (October 1993), pp. 109–112.

INDEX